The BIG ALABAMA REPRODUCIBLE Activity Book!

BY CAROLE MARSH

This activity book has material which correlates with the Alabama Course of Study for Social Studies.

At every opportunity, we have tried to relate information to the Alabama History and Social Science, English, Science, Math, Civics, Economics, and Computer Technology directives.

For additional information, go to our websites:
www.alabamaexperience.com or **www.gallopade.com**.

Published by

800-536-2GET
www.gallopade.com

Gallopade is proud to be a member or supporter of these educational organizations and associations:

A Word From The Author

Alabama is a very special state. Almost everything about Alabama is interesting and fun! It has a remarkable history that helped create the great nation of America. Alabama enjoys an amazing geography of incredible beauty and fascination. The state's people are unique and have accomplished many great things.

This Activity Book is chock-full of activities to entice you to learn more about Alabama. While completing puzzles, coloring activities, word codes, and other fun-to-do activities, you'll learn about the state's history, geography, people, places, animals, legends, and more.

Whether you're sitting in a classroom, stuck inside on a rainy day, or—better yet—sitting in the back seat of a car touring the wonderful state of Alabama, my hope is that you have as much fun using this Activity Book as I did writing it.

Enjoy your Alabama Experience—it's the trip of a lifetime!!

Carole Marsh

The Alabama Experience Series

The BIG Alabama Wall Timeline

Alabama Student Reference Timeline

My First Pocket Guide to Alabama!

The Alabama Coloring Book!

My First Book About Alabama!

Alabama Jeopardy: Answers and Questions About Our State

Alabama "Jography!": A Fun Run Through Our State

The Alabama Experience! Sticker Pack

The Alabama Experience! Poster/Map

Discover Alabama CD-ROM

Alabama "HISTORY" Bingo Game

Alabama "GEOGRAPHY" Bingo Game

Alabama "BIOGRAPHY" Bingo Game

Color Me!

BROWN
Brown like crunchy pecans, the state nut.
Brown

BLUE
Blue like the clear sky where space shuttles blast off in Huntsville.
Blue

YELLOW
Yellow like the golden-winged woodpecker (yellowhammer), the state bird.
Yellow

RED
Red like the bold cross of St. Andrew on the state flag.
Red

BLACK
Black like the inky stripes of a zebra living at the Montgomery Zoo.
Black

PURPLE
Purple like the exciting Alabama Renaissance Faire in Florence.
Purple

GREEN
Green like the crawling state reptile, the Alabama red-bellied turtle.
Green

ORANGE
Orange like the velvety wings of a monarch butterfly, the state insect.
Orange

ALABAMA

Geographic Tools

Beside each geographic need listed, put the initials of the tool that can best help you!

(CR) Compass Rose   (LL) Longitude and Latitude
(M) Map   (G) Grid
(K) Map key/legend

1. _____ I need to find the geographic location of Germany.

2. _____ I need to learn where an airport is located near Bessemer.

3. _____ I need to find which way is north.

4. _____ I need to chart a route from Alabama to California.

5. _____ I need to find a small town on a map.

Match the items on the left with the items on the right.

1. Grid system   A. Map key or legend

2. Compass rose   B. Georgia and Mississippi

3. Longitude and latitude C. A system of letters and numbers

4. Two of Alabama(s) borders D. Imaginary lines around the earth

5. Symbols on a map   E. Shows N, S, E, and W

ANSWERS: 1-LL; 2-K; 3-CR, 4-M; 5-G; 1-C; 2-E; 3-D; 4-B; 5-A

Is It Fact Or Fiction?

Harper Lee was born in 1926 and lived in the town of Monroeville. Her father was an attorney who had plans for her to join his law firm. But this was not to be. Although Harper Lee studied law, she became a writer instead and created one of the most powerful novels ever written—*To Kill a Mockingbird.*

The story and characters were inspired by events and people in her life and told of the turmoil and racial tension in the South. One case that impacted her novel was the Scottsboro Case, in which nine African Americans were falsely accused of attacking white women on a train.

The narrator and main character in *To Kill a Mockingbird* is Scout. Along with the rest of her small Southern town, Scout watches as Atticus, her father the attorney, defends an African American man falsely accused of attacking a white girl. Scout comes to see and understand her father in many new ways as the story of *To Kill a Mockingbird* unfolds.

Read each sentence, and decide if it is FACT or FICTION. Write your answers on the lines provided.

1. Harper Lee was born in 1926 and lived in Monroeville.

   _____

2. Harper Lee studied law but became a writer.

   _____

3. The story of *To Kill a Mockingbird* was partly inspired by the Scottsboro Case.

   _____

4. Scout's father, Atticus, is a doctor.

   _____

5. Scout learns many new things about her mother.

   _____

ANSWERS: 1-fact; 2-fact; 3-fact; 4-fiction; 5-fiction

Alabama Government

Alabama's state government, just like our national government, is made up of three branches. Each branch has a certain job to do. Each branch also has some power over the other branches. We call this system checks and balances. The three branches work together to make our government work smoothly.

Two Houses: The Senate (35 members) House of Representatives (105 members)	A governor, lieutenant governor, secretary of state, state treasurer, attorney general, auditor, and commissioner of Agriculture and Industries	Supreme Court (9 members) Court of Civil Appeals Court of Criminal Appeals Circuit Courts District Courts Probate Courts Municipal Courts
Legislative Branch	**Executive Branch**	**Judicial Branch**

For each of these government officials, circle whether he or she is part of the EXECUTIVE, the LEGISLATIVE, or the JUDICIAL branch.

1.	Governor	EXECUTIVE	LEGISLATIVE	JUDICIAL
2.	Civil Appeals Court Judge	EXECUTIVE	LEGISLATIVE	JUDICIAL
3.	State Treasurer	EXECUTIVE	LEGISLATIVE	JUDICIAL
4.	State Representatives	EXECUTIVE	LEGISLATIVE	JUDICIAL
5.	Supreme Court Justice	EXECUTIVE	LEGISLATIVE	JUDICIAL
6.	Auditor	EXECUTIVE	LEGISLATIVE	JUDICIAL
7.	Lt. Governor	EXECUTIVE	LEGISLATIVE	JUDICIAL
8.	District Court Judge	EXECUTIVE	LEGISLATIVE	JUDICIAL
9.	Attorney General	EXECUTIVE	LEGISLATIVE	JUDICIAL
10.	State Senator	EXECUTIVE	LEGISLATIVE	JUDICIAL

The number of legislators may change after each census.

ANSWERS: 1-Executive; 2-Judicial; 3-Executive; 4-Legislative; 5-Judicial; 6-Executive; 7-Executive; 8-Judicial; 9-Executive; 10-Legislative

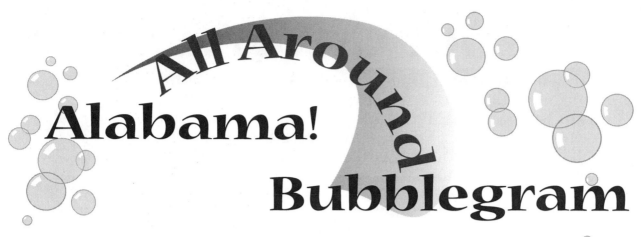

All Around
Alabama!
Bubblegram

Fill in the bubblegram by using the clues below.

1. A state to the north
2. A state to the south
3. A state to the west
4. A state to the east

1. __ ○ __ __ __ __ __ __ __ __

2. __ __ __ __ __ __ __ ○

3. __ __ __ __ __ __ __ __ __ __ __

4. __ __ __ ○ __ __ __

Now unscramble the "bubble" letters to find out the mystery words!

Mystery Message:
One of Alabama's nicknames is "THE H __ __ __T OF DIXIE"

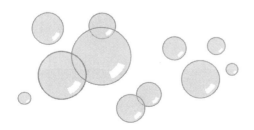

According To Alabama Legends...

A rebus is a picture puzzle. **Use the picture clues in this rebus to learn about some old Alabama legends.**

1. If [sheep] have a [lamp] + [boy pulling wagon] + N + your + CH + [cube with arrow] , + [two hikers] + Y + [hearts] + U + [paper with pen] + [running man] =

If _ _ _ have a _ _ _ _ _ _ _ _ your _ _ _ _ , _ _ _ _
_ _ _ _ _ _ _ _ _ _ _ _ _ _ _ !

2. If a [caterpillar] − [column] + [man sneezing AH CHOO] + [baseball player] a [beach] + [hand writing Name] + [ON OFF switch] + [sun/cloud]

+ N! = If a _ _ _ _ _ _ _ _ _ _ , _ _ ' _ a _ _ _ _ _
_ _ _ _ _ _ _ _ _ _ !

3. If + U + C + a + D + [red crayon] − r + [frog] , + [hand drawing figures] +
a + [circus tent] − cus + cle + around + [baseball player] , + s p + [baseball player] + [ON OFF switch] + [baseball player] ,
a n d + m + 8 + [birthday cake] − c + a [fish] − f + w! Then ... = If
_ _ _ _ _ _ a _ _ _ _ _ _ _ _ _ , _ _ _ _

a _ _ _ _ _ _ _ around _ _ , _ _ _ _ _ _ _ _ _ , and

_ _ _ _ _ a _ _ _ _ ! Then your wish will come true!

Alabama Wheel of Fortune, Indian Style!

The names of Alabama's many Native American tribes contain enough consonants to play . . . Wheel of Fortune!

See if you can figure out the Wheel of Fortune-style puzzles below! "Vanna" has given you some of the consonants in each word.

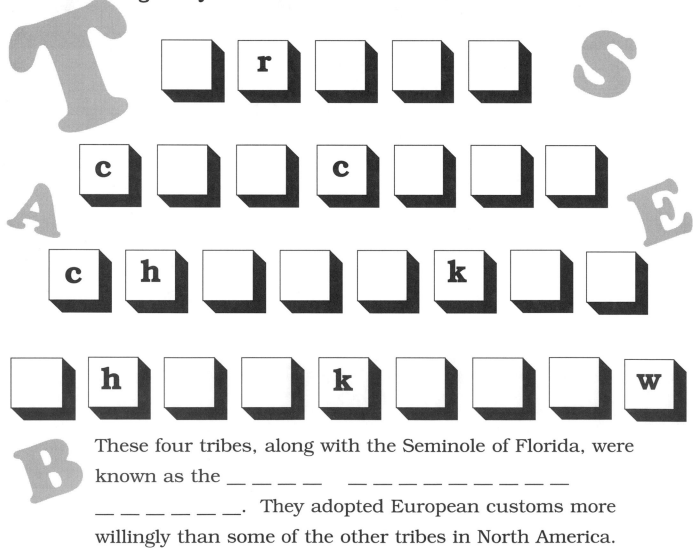

These four tribes, along with the Seminole of Florida, were known as the _ _ _ _   _ _ _ _ _ _ _ _ _ _ _ _ _ _. They adopted European customs more willingly than some of the other tribes in North America.

Rainbow, Pretty Rainbow

Rainbows often appear over Mobile Bay after a storm. Rainbows are formed when sunlight bends through raindrops. Big raindrops produce the brightest, most beautiful rainbows. You can see rainbows early or late on a rainy day when the sun is behind you.

Color the rainbow in the order the colors are listed below, starting at the top of the rainbow. Then, in each band write down as many Alabama-related words as you can think of that begin with the same first letter as that color!

Rainbow Colors

Red
Orange
Yellow
Green
Blue
Purple

In the Beginning...
Came a Colony

The first explorers to arrive in present-day Alabama were the Spanish. Some explorers traveled over land. Some sailed their boats through the Gulf of Mexico into Mobile Bay. They came looking for new lands to conquer and golden treasures to keep!

Help the Spanish find their way to Alabama!

Mobile Bay

Finish

Start

U.S. Time Zones

Would you believe that the contiguous United States is divided into four time zones? It is! Because of the rotation of the earth, the sun appears to travel from east to west. Whenever the sun is directly overhead, we call that time noon. When it is noon in Birmingham, the sun has a long way to go before it is directly over San Francisco, California. When it is 12:00 p.m. (noon) in Montgomery, it is 11:00 a.m. in Denver, Colorado. There is a one-hour time difference between each zone!

Look at the time zones on the map below then answer the following questions:

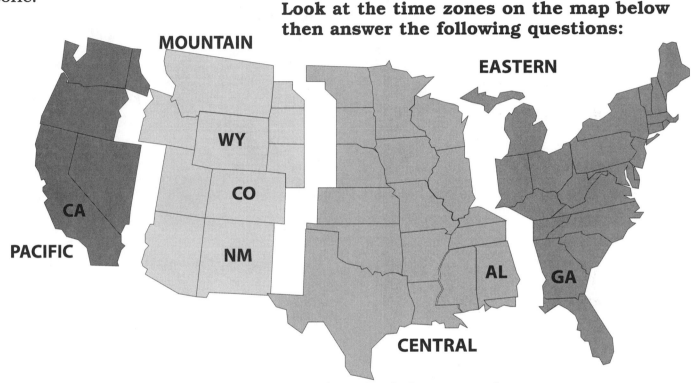

1. When it is 10:00 a.m. in Dothan, Alabama, what time is it in California? _____ a.m.

2. When it is 3:30 p.m. in Atlanta, Georgia, what time is it in Alabama? _____ p.m.

3. In what time zone is Alabama located? _____

4. In what time zone is Colorado located? _____

5. If it is 10:00 p.m. in Decatur, Alabama, what time is it in Wyoming? _____ p.m.

ANSWERS: 1-8:00 a.m.; 2-2:30 p.m.; 3-Central; 4-Mountain; 5-9:00 p.m.

Sing Like a Alabama Bird Word Jumble

Arrange the jumbled letters in the proper order for the names of birds found in Alabama.

BIRD BANK

Blackbird
Cardinal
Crow
Goldfinch
Mockingbird
Owl
Robin
Sparrow
Woodpecker
Yellowhammer
(state bird)

eyllwoahmmre _ _ _ _ _ _ _ _ _ _ _

rowspar _ _ _ _ _ _ _

oodwkerpec _ _ _ _ _ _ _ _ _ _

low _ _ _

rowc _ _ _ _

binro _ _ _ _ _

birdingcomk _ _ _ _ _ _ _ _ _ _ _

lanidrca _ _ _ _ _ _ _ _

inchfdolg _ _ _ _ _ _ _ _ _

lcbrbakid _ _ _ _ _ _ _ _ _

©2004 Carole Marsh/Gallopade International/800-536-2GET/www.alabamaexperience.com/Page 14

Alabama Schools Rule!

The state school system of Alabama was established in 1854. Today there are about 130 public school systems. Law requires that all children ages seven to 15 go to school! Alabama has private schools, junior colleges, technical institutes, and universities located throughout the state. There's even a school run by the U.S. government—the Community College of the Air Force at Maxwell Air Force base in Montgomery!

Complete the names of these Alabama schools. Use the Word Bank to help you. Then, use the answers to solve the code at the bottom.

WORD BANK

Auburn	South
Huntingdon	Spring Hill
Jacksonville	Troy
North	Tuskegee University
Samford	University of Alabama

1. _ _ _ _ _ _ University in Auburn and Montgomery
   7

2. _ _ _ _ _ _ _ _ _   _ _ _ _ _ _ _ _ _ _

3. _ _ _ _ _ _ _ _ _ _   _ _   _ _ _ _ _ _ _
   4
   in Birmingham, Huntsville, and Tuscaloosa

4. _ _ _ _ _ _ _ _ _ _ _ College in Montgomery
   1

5. _ _ _ _ _ _ _ _ _ _ _ _ State University

6. Troy State University in _ _ _ _ , Dothan, and Montgomery

7. University of _ _ _ _ _ Alabama in Florence
   5

8. University of _ _ _ _ _ Alabama in Mobile

9. _ _ _ _ _ _ _ University in Birmingham
   6

10. _ _ _ _ _ _   _ _ _ _ College in Mobile
    2

The coded message tells you what all college students want!

_ _ P _ _ _ _
1 2 3 4 5 6 7

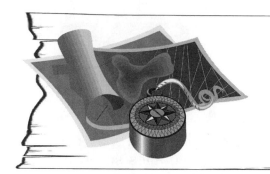

Alabama Topography is "Tops"!

Beginning in the Appalachian Mountains (the Cumberland or Appalachian Plateau) in the northeast, Alabama gently slopes to the Bay of Mobile (the East Gulf Coastal Plain) in the southwest.

In east-central Alabama lies the Piedmont with low hills and high ridges. The rich, black soil of the Black Belt stretches from west-central to the middle of the coastal plain.

Starting with the first, cross out every other letter below to figure out the geographical term.

1. **A G W O C R K G L E**: a deep, narrow passage between mountains =

_____

2. **X B Z A E S E I T N**: a large hollow, often filled with water =

_____

3. **Z V C A E L A L N E M Y**: low land lying between hills or mountains =

_____

4. **B R E I Q D C G S E**: long, narrow elevation of land =

_____

5. **P F E L B A A T P L C A L N Q D**: expanse of land that does not vary in height above sea level =

_____

6. **T M Q O W U R N I T S A V I T N U S**: chain or group of very high hills =

_____

7. **F H G I A L B L T S**: ground higher than the land around it, but not as high as mountains =

_____

8. **P T A O Y P U O M G Q R T A O P V H K Y**: the detailed mapping of the features on the surface of land =

_____

ANSWERS: 1-gorge; 2-basin; 3-valley; 4-ridge; 5-flatland; 6-mountains; 7-hills; 8-topography

Oh! Say Can You See... The Alabama State Flag

Alabama's *current* state flag was adopted in 1895. It features the crimson cross of St. Andrew on a field of white.

The *first* state flag was adopted in 1861 and is known as the Republic of Alabama flag. The Goddess of Liberty stood tall with a sword in her right hand and a small flag with one star in the left. **Color the state flag.**

Fast Facts

As you travel throughout Alabama, count the times you see the Alabama flag! Look for it on government vehicles, too!

The Republic of Alabama flag flew until 1891. It was damaged in a storm and retired. It never flew again!

Design your own Diamante on Alabama!

A *diamante* is a cool diamond-shaped poem on any subject.

You can write your very own diamante poem on Alabama by following the simple line by line directions below. Give it a try!

Line 1: Write the name of the state.

Line 2: Write the names of two animals native to Alabama.

Line 3: Write the names of three cities in Alabama.

Line 4: Write the names of four of Alabama's agricultural products.

Line 5: Write the names of three Alabama birds.

Line 6: Write the names of Alabama's state insect and state flower.

Line 7: Write the word that completes this sentence:

Alabama is known as the _____ State.

_____

_____ _____

_____ _____ _____

_____ _____ _____ _____

_____ _____ _____

_____ _____

_____

YOU'RE a poet!
Did you know it?

History Mystery Tour

Alabama is bursting at the seams with history! Here are just a few of the many historical sites that you might visit! Try your hand at locating them on the map!

Draw the symbol for each site on the Alabama map below.

State Capitol, Montgomery—colonial-style building, built in 1850-1851 with later additions; bronze star marks spot where Jefferson Davis took oath of office as president of the Confederate States of America

Alabama Constitution Village, Huntsville—commemorates location of 1819 Constitutional Convention

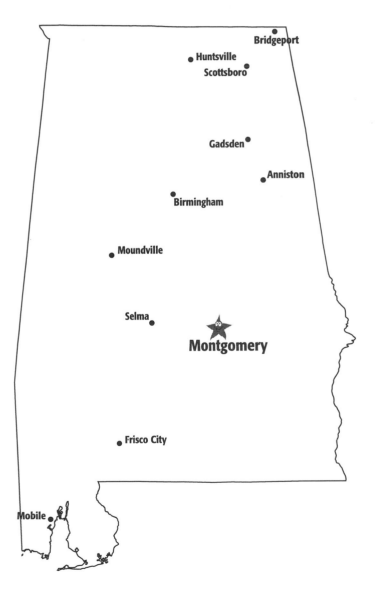

Martin Luther King, Jr. Street, Selma—memorials highlight history of voting rights movement

Russell Cave National Monument, Bridgeport—one of longest and most complete archaeological records in eastern United States; contains prehistoric artifacts and skeleton of prehistoric man

What in the World?

A hemisphere is one-half of a sphere (globe) created by the prime meridian or equator. Every place in the world is in two hemispheres (Northern or Southern and Eastern or Western). The equator is an imaginary line that runs around the world from left to right and divides the globe into the Northern Hemisphere and the Southern Hemisphere. The prime meridian is an imaginary line that runs around the world from top to bottom and divides the globe into the Eastern Hemisphere and Western Hemisphere.

Label the Northern and Southern Hemispheres.

Write E on the equator.

Is Alabama in the NORTHERN or SOUTHERN Hemisphere? (circle one)

Color the map.

Label the Eastern and Western Hemispheres.

Write PM on the prime meridian.

Is Alabama in the EASTERN or WESTERN Hemisphere? (circle one)

Color the map.

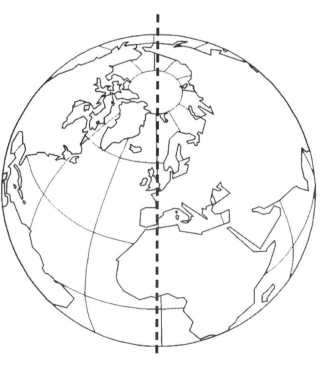

ANSWERS: Northern; Western

Places to go!
Things to do!

Alabama has so many cool places to go and so many cool things to do! **Use the Word Bank to help you complete the sentences below and learn about some of the exciting Alabama sites you can visit!**

1. _ _ _ _ _ _ _ _ _ _ _ _ _ _ _ _ _ _ National Historic Site

2. _ _ _ _ _ _ State Park—one of deepest canyons east of the Mississippi River

3. W.C. Handy Home and Museum in _ _ _ _ _ _ _ _ is the birthplace of blues composer W.C. Handy; includes handwritten music, trumpet, and piano on which he wrote "St. Louis Blues."

4. Huntsville _ _ _ _ _ _ _ _ _ Garden—woodland paths, meadows, aquatic area

5. _ _ _ _ _ _ _ _ _ _ _ _ _ _, Haleys—longest natural bridge east of Rocky Mountains

6. _ _ _ _ _ _ _ _ _ _ _ _ _, Phil Campbell—was once a ceremonial ground for Native Americans and a hideout for outlaws; caves, waterfalls, forests, craggy rock formations, rainbows, and phosphorescent creatures called "dismalites" that glow in the dark; National Natural Landmark

7. Anniston Museum of _ _ _ _ _ _ _ _ _ _ _ _ _ _ has dinosaurs, fossils, Egyptian mummies, and more on exhibit.

8. _ _ _ _ _ _ _ _ _ _ _ _ _ _ _ _ _ _ _ _ Historical State Park, Civil War Site—built in 1862; produced iron for Confederate weapons

WORD BANK			
Botanical	Brierfield Ironworks	DeSoto	Dismals Canyon
Florence	Natural Bridge	Natural History	Tuskegee Institute

Please Come to Alabama!

You have a friend who lives in Wyoming. She is thinking of moving to Alabama because she wants to be an astronaut, and Alabama is *the* place to learn how to climb aboard a shuttle and launch into space to explore the final frontier.

Write her a letter describing Alabama and some of the aeronautical opportunities there. Tell your friend about Rocket City, USA!

Fast Facts

The George C. Marshall Space Flight Center in Huntsville was the first headquarters of NASA, the National Aeronautics and Space Administration. Huntsville and its research labs, assembly plants, and launch pads became known as Rocket City, USA!

A Time of Battles, Bravery, And Blood

The Civil War was fought between the American states from 1861 to 1865. The argument was over states' rights to make their own decisions, including whether or not to own slaves. Southern states, with plantations and slaves, were on one side of this conflict. Northern states, which opposed slavery or had no need of it, were on the other side. Some of the southern states began to secede (leave) the Union. They formed the Confederate States of America. Montgomery was selected to be the first Confederate capital and became known as the "Cradle of the Confederacy."

After four long years, the Confederacy surrendered at Appomattox Court House in Virginia. It took years for the country to recover from the devastation of this unfortunate war, in which Americans could find no way to agree, except to fight!

Take a crossword-puzzle tour of Alabama's Civil War battle sites.

Fast Fact

More Americans were killed during the Civil War than during World Wars I and II together!

Fast Fact

Soldiers who did survive the war often went home without an arm, leg, or both, since amputation was the "cure" for most battlefield wounds.

WORD BANK

Athens
Decatur
Mobile Bay
Days Gap
Fort Blakeley
Selma
Spanish Fort

ANSWERS: Across: 1-Selma; 5-Fort Blakeley; 6-Athens; Down: 2-Mobile Bay; 3-Days Gap (apostrophe removed); 4-Decatur; 7-Spanish Fort

Alabama Rules!

The Civil Rights Act of 1964 banned discrimination on the basis of color, race, national origin, religion or sex; guaranteed equal access to public facilities, the right to vote, and employment opportunities.

Fast Facts

Dr. Martin Luther King, Jr. led thousands in a march from Selma to Montgomery to protest unjust obstacles that kept African Americans from registering to vote. The Voting Rights Act of 1965 banned the unfair poll tax, literacy test, and property requirements.

Use the code to complete the sentences.

A	B	C	D	E	F	G	H	I	J	K	L	M	N	O	P
1	2	3	4	5	6	7	8	9	10	11	12	13	14	15	16

Q	R	S	T	U	V	W	X	Y	Z
17	18	19	20	21	22	23	24	25	26

1. State rules are called __ __ __ __.
                   12 1 23 19

2. Laws are made in our state __ __ __ __ __ __ __.
                   3 1 16 9 20 15 12

3. The leader of our state is the __ __ __ __ __ __ __ __.
                   7 15 22 5 18 14 15 18

4. We live in the state of __ __ __ __ __ __ __.
                   1 12 1 2 1 13 1

5. The capital of our state is __ __ __ __ __ __ __ __ __ __.
                   13 15 14 20 7 15 13 5 18 25

ANSWERS: 1-laws; 2-capitol; 3-governor; 4-Alabama; 5-Montgomery

Buzzing Around Alabama!

Write the answers to the questions below. To get to the beehive, follow a path through the maze.

1. Monte Sano State Park has a large deep, circular hole (How deep? No one knows!): _ _ _ _ _ _ _ _ _ _ _

2. Home of Walter and Bessie Bellingrath, Mobile's first Coca-Cola bottlers: _ _ _ _ _ _ _ _ _ _ _ Gardens and Home, Theodore

3. Helen Keller was born here: _ _ _ _ _ _ _ _, Tuscumbia

4. One of the last Confederate forts to fall to Union forces: Fort Morgan State Historic Site in _ _ _ _ _ _ _ _ _ _

5. Site where General Andrew Jackson defeated Creek Nation: _ _ _ _ _ _ _ _ _ _ _ _ _ National Military Park, Daviston

6. Site of last major Civil War battle: _ _ _ _ _ _ _ _ _ _ _, Historic Blakeley State Park

7. Outstanding references on history and culture of Alabama: _ _ _ _ _ _ _ _ _ _ _ _ _ _ _ _ _ _ _ Library, University of Alabama

8. Spectacular canyon is one of the deepest gorges east of Mississippi River: _ _ _ _ _ _ _ _ _ _ _ _ _ _ _ _ _ _ _ National Preserve, Blanche

9. Museum commemorates success of local country music band: _ _ _ _ _ _ _ Fan Club and Museum, Fort Payne

10. Museum commemorates Alabama's greatest sports legends; displays original memorabilia from more than 180 members: Alabama _ _ _ _ _ _ Hall of Fame, Birmingham; honorees include Coach Paul "Bear" Bryant, Joe Louis, Jesse Owens, Joe Namath, Bobby Allison, and Jennifer Chandler-Jones

WORD BANK

ALABAMA
Bellingrath
Amelia Gayle Gorgas
Gulf Shores
Horseshoe Bend
Ivy Green
Little River Canyon
Natural Well
Spanish Fort
Sports

Maze hexagons: Start here, Natural Well, Ivy Green, Bellingrath, Gulf Shores, ALABAMA, Little River Canyon, Sports, Amelia Gayle Gorgas, Horseshoe Bend, Spanish Fort

ANSWERS: 1-Natural Well; 2-Bellingrath; 3-Ivy Green; 4-Gulf Shores; 5-Horseshoe Bend; 6-Spanish Fort; 7-Amelia Gayle Gorgas; 8-Little River Canyon; 9-ALABAMA; 10-Sports

Alabama Through the Years!

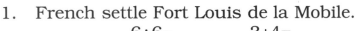

Many great things have happened in Alabama throughout its history.

Chronicle the following important Alabama events by solving math problems to find out the years in which they happened.

1. French settle Fort Louis de la Mobile.
    $6 \div 6 =$ $3 + 4 =$ $2 - 2 =$ $9 - 7 =$

2. Treaty of Paris ends French and Indian War, France gives Alabama to England.
    $5 \div 5 =$ $9 - 2 =$ $2 \times 3 =$ $9 - 6 =$

3. Spain captures Mobile.
    $2 - 1 =$ $5 + 2 =$ $2 \times 4 =$ $6 - 6 =$

4. England cedes northern part of Alabama to United States and cedes Mobile region to Spain.
    $1 + 0 =$ $3 + 4 =$ $10 - 2 =$ $6 - 3 =$

5. U.S. Congress organizes the Alabama Territory.
    $8 - 7 =$ $4 \times 2 =$ $10 - 9 =$ $4 + 3 =$

6. Alabama joins Union, becomes 22nd state.
    $8 \div 8 =$ $7 + 1 =$ $4 - 3 =$ $6 + 3 =$

7. Alabama secedes from the Union, becomes the Republic of Alabama for a short time, then joins the Confederate States of America; Civil War begins.
    $1 + 0 =$ $5 + 3 =$ $6 + 0 =$ $8 - 7 =$

8. Confederacy surrenders to the Union; Civil War ends.
    $7 - 6 =$ $4 + 4 =$ $3 + 3 =$ $5 + 0 =$

9. Alabama is readmitted to the Union.
    $1 \times 0 =$ $4 \times 2 =$ $3 \times 2 =$ $2 \times 4 =$

10. Present state constitution is adopted.
    $3 - 2 =$ $4 + 5 =$ $1 - 1 =$ $5 - 4 =$

ANSWERS: 1-1702; 2-1763; 3-1780; 4-1783; 5-1817; 6-1819; 7-1861; 8-1865; 9-1868; 10-1901

What Did We Do Before Money?

In early Alabama, there were no banks. However, people still wanted to barter, trade, or otherwise "purchase" goods from each other. Wampum, made of shells, bone, or stones, was often swapped for goods. Indians, especially, used wampum for "money." In the barter system, people swapped goods or services.

Later, banks came into existence, and people began to use money to buy goods. However, they also still bartered when they had no money to spend.

Alabama's early economy was based on agriculture with cotton leading the way! After the Civil War, Alabama's economy was in terrible shape. The iron and steel industries in northern Alabama boosted the state's financial status toward the end of the 19th century!

Place a star in the box below the systems used today.

Rhymin' Riddles

1. I am a southern state and my name *starts* with an "A"!

   I am that southern state and my name *ends* with an "A"!

   What am I? _____

2. I came to this land from across the sea;

   Led a colony for three years, but it wasn't to be!

   Who am I? _____

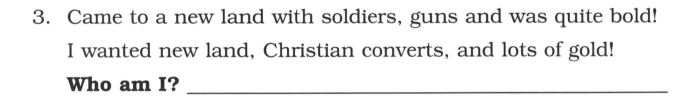

3. Came to a new land with soldiers, guns and was quite bold!

   I wanted new land, Christian converts, and lots of gold!

   Who am I? _____

4. We built the first settlement named Fort Louis de la Mobile.

   We came, we saw, and we settled—*with zeal!*

   Who are we? _____

ANSWERS: 1-Alabama; 2-Tristán de Luna; 3-Hernando de Soto; 4-French

 # Map Symbols

Make up symbols for these names and draw them in the space provided on the right.

mountain	
river	
lake	
battlefield	
airport	
train	
capital	
iron works	
state gem	

Alabama Goodies!

Match the name of each crop or product from Alabama with the picture of that item.

| Soybeans | Peanuts | Corn |
| Wheat | Cotton | Pecans |

Fast Facts

Cotton ruled as "King" through the 19th century! It was Alabama's cash crop and economic support!

At the beginning of the 20th century, 90 percent of Alabama's population made their living as farmers.

Today, cotton is still an important crop, but service industries have replaced agriculture as Alabama's main industry!

Historical Alabama Women World Wonders!

Alabama has been the home of many brave and influential women. See if you can match these women with their accomplishments.

1. _____ Rosa Parks
2. _____ Julia Strudwick Tutwiler
3. _____ Lurleen Burns Wallace
4. _____ Mae Jemison
5. _____ Jennifer Chandler-Jones

6. _____ Fannie Flagg
7. _____ Nora Ezell
8. _____ Lomia Nunn
9. _____ Gail Thrower
10. _____ Heather Whitestone

A. Poarch Creek Native American, serves as tribal historian/ librarian on reservation near Atmore; only granddaughter of the last tribal medicine man; gives talks and demonstrations on Creek heritage to schools and other groups; received Alabama Folk Heritage Award

B. Diver, Olympic gold medal winner

C. First African American woman astronaut, launched into space aboard the shuttle *Endeavor*

D. Miss America of 1995, first Miss America chosen with a disability; she is deaf

E. Author, wrote *Fried Green Tomatoes at the Whistle Stop Cafe*; movie, *Fried Green Tomatoes* based on her book

F. Quilt maker; uses traditional wedding ring, log cabin, and bear's paw patterns as well as her own innovative storytelling designs; has received numerous awards including National Heritage Fellowship and Alabama Folk Heritage Award

G. Traditional basketmaker; learned art of basketmaking from her father who made cotton baskets for farmers; received Alabama Folk Heritage Award

H. Educator and social reformer; helped establish many girls' schools and successfully fought for women to be admitted to the University of Alabama; worked for prison reform; wrote the words to "Alabama," the state song; honoree in the Alabama Women's Hall of Fame

I. A very brave lady who took a major step toward integration and civil rights. After a long day at work, she took a seat on a bus, but she wouldn't give it up to a white man as the law of segregation required. She was arrested, leading to a year-long boycott of Montgomery buses.

J. First woman governor of Alabama; honoree in the Alabama Women's Hall of Fame

ANSWERS: 1-I, 2-H, 3-J, 4-C; 5-B; 6-E; 7-F; 8-G; 9-A; 10-D

Producers and Consumers

Producers (sellers) make goods or provide services. Ralph, a fourth grade student in Tuscaloosa, is a consumer because he wants to buy a new wheel for his bicycle. Other Alabama products and services for consumers include paper products, textiles, clothing, seafood, petroleum, retail sales, financial services, insurance, and real estate.

Tourism (a service) brings in more than $3 billion to Alabama's economy every year. Shipping is an important part of the state's economy. The port of Mobile is a major distribution point for coal and petroleum products.

Complete these sentences.

Without notebook paper, I couldn't

_____

_____

Without a tour guide, I couldn't

_____

_____

Without towels, I couldn't

_____

_____

Without a bank, I couldn't

_____

_____

Alabama Word Wheel!

Use the Word Wheel of Alabama names to complete the sentences below.

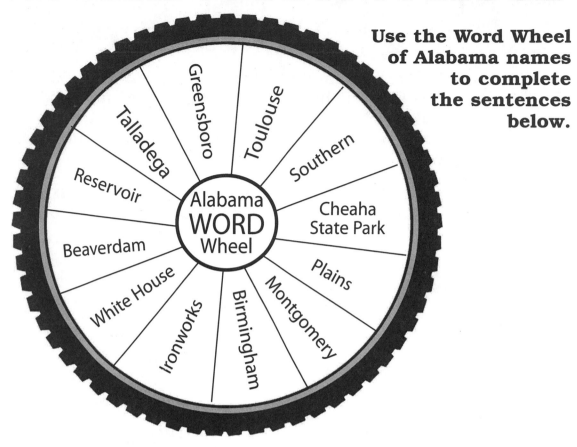

Alabama WORD Wheel

Greensboro • Toulouse • Southern • Cheaha State Park • Plains • Montgomery • Birmingham • Ironworks • White House • Beaverdam • Reservoir • Talladega

1. _____ _____ _____ in Talladega National Forest contains Cheaha Mountain, Alabama's highest peak.
2. First _____ _____ of the Confederacy in Montgomery was the home of Confederate President and Mrs. Jefferson Davis.
3. Magnolia Grove in _____ is an antebellum mansion and the birthplace of Rear Admiral Richmond Pearson Hobson.
4. Fort _____, Jackson National Historic Park in Wetumpka, was built by General Andrew Jackson following the defeat of Creek Nation.
5. _____'s Department of Archives and History was the nation's first library to become part of a state government.
6. Botanical Gardens in _____ is one of the largest publicly-owned botanical gardens in the United States.
7. _____ Creek Swamp in Decatur is a pure tupelo gum tree swamp located in Wheeler National Wildlife Refuge. It's a National Natural Landmark!
8. _____ Museum of Flight in Birmingham remembers 80 years of aviation history, including achievements of the Tuskegee Airmen.
9. Tannehill _____ Historic State Park in McCalla is a living history park surrounding ironworks destroyed by Union raid in 1865.
10. International Motorsports Hall of Fame in _____ where more than 100 racing vehicles and memorabilia dating back to 1902 are on display.

The Roads Well Traveled!

   Alabama's major interstate highways include I-20, I-59, I-78, I-65, I-85, I-231, and I-10. A state highway department was established in 1911, but before then, private companies built the roads that took Alabamians where they needed to go! Today, Alabama has approximately 100,000 miles (161,000 kilometers) of roads and highways.

Using the map below to help you, write down the direction you'd travel and the highway you'd take in order to get from:

1. Athens to Montgomery =

   _____

2. Auburn to Tuskegee =

   _____

3. Leeds to Oxford =

   _____

4. Daphne to Mobile =

   _____

Bridgeport
Russell Cave National Monument
Athens
Huntsville
Tennessee River
Gilliland-Reese Covered Bridge
65
59
Gadsen
Jacksonville State University
Church of St. Michael and All Angels
Anniston
Pell City
20
Oxford
Birmingham
Leeds
Talladega Superspeedway
Black Warrior River
Lake Logan Martin
Coosa River
Lake Martin
Tuscaloosa
59
Auburn
20
Museum of Fine Arts
85
Tuskegee
Tombigee River
Montgomery
Alabama River
65
231
Oakleigh Period Museum House
Mobile
10
Daphne

ANSWERS: 1–south on I-65; 2–southeast on I-85; 3–east on I-20; 4–northwest on I-10

Create Your Own Alabama State Quarter!

Look at the change in your pocket. You might notice that one of the coins has changed. The United States is minting new quarters, one for each of the 50 states. Each quarter has a design on it that says something special about one particular state. The Alabama quarter will be in cash registers and piggy banks everywhere after it's released in 2003.

What if you had designed the Alabama quarter? Draw a picture of how you would like the Alabama quarter to look. Make sure you include things that are special about Alabama.

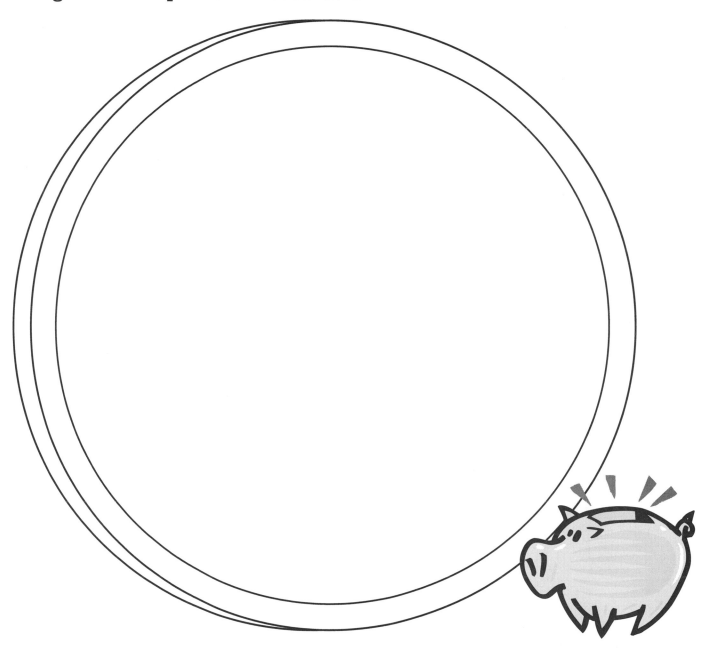

Alabama Law Comes In Many Flavors!

For each of these people, write down the kind(s) of law used to decide whether their actions are legal or illegal.

1. Bank robber _____

2. Business person _____

3. State park ranger _____

4. Alabamians _____

5. Doctor _____

6. Real estate agent _____

7. Corporate president _____

8. Ship owner _____

9. Diplomat _____

10. Soldier _____

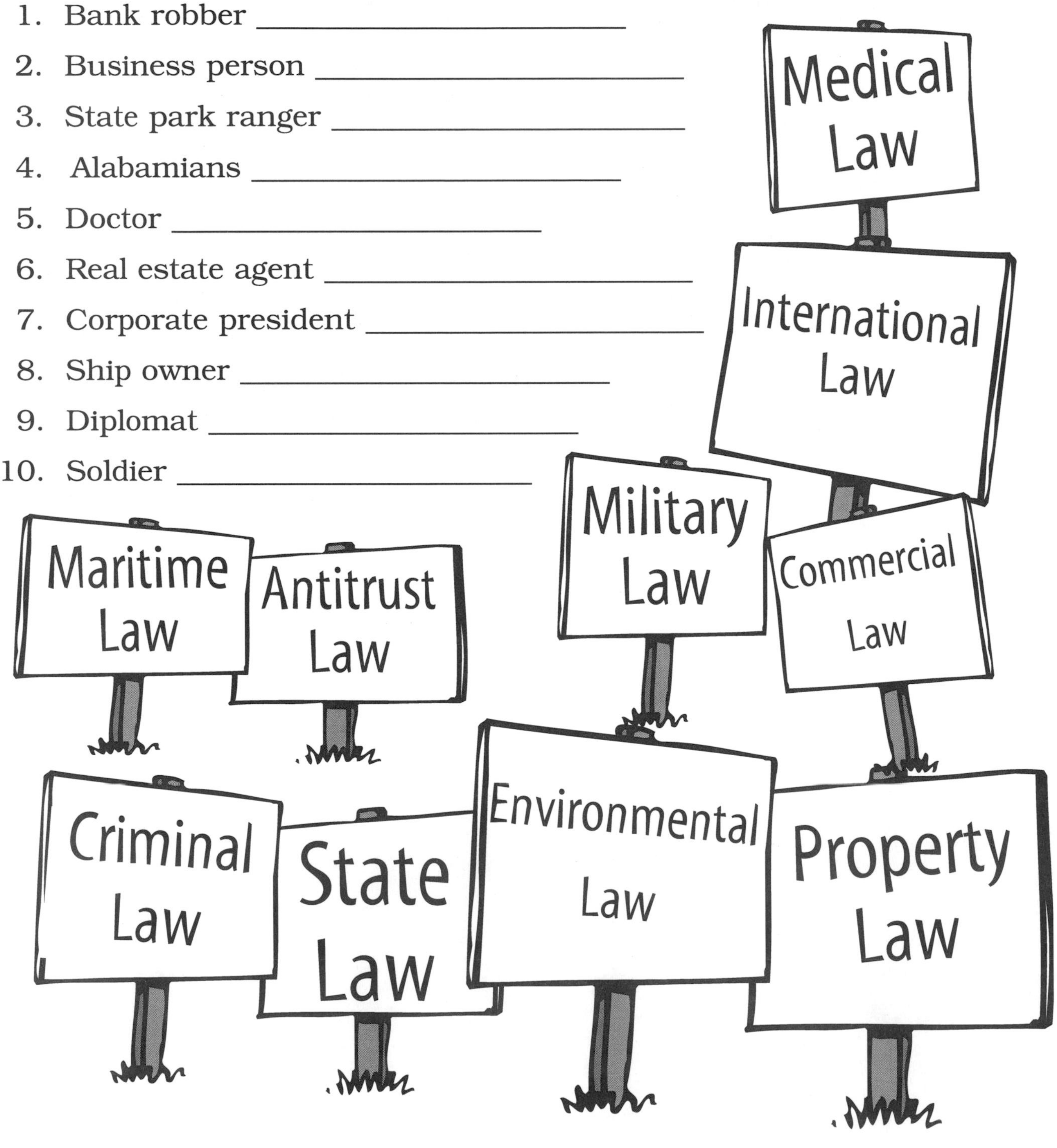

Medical Law

International Law

Military Law

Commercial Law

Maritime Law

Antitrust Law

Criminal Law

State Law

Environmental Law

Property Law

ANSWERS: (Answers may vary.) 1–Criminal; 2–Commercial; 3–Environmental; 4–State; 5–Medical; 6–Property; 7–Antitrust; 8–Maritime; 9–International; 10–Military.

Mixed-Up States!

Color, cut out, and paste each of Alabama's four neighbors onto the map below.

Be sure and match the state shapes!

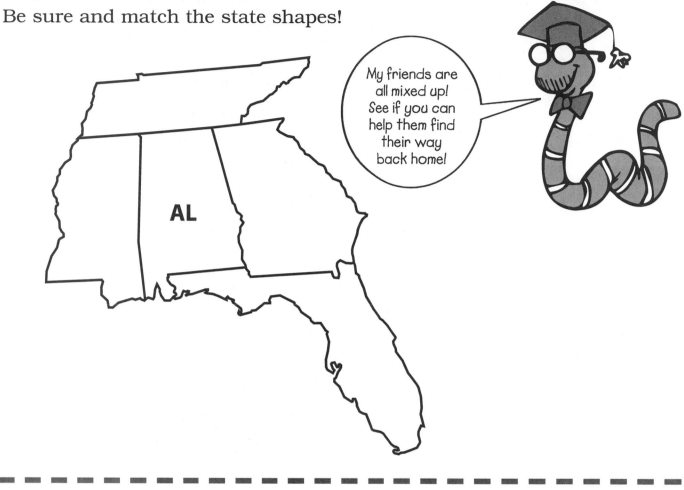

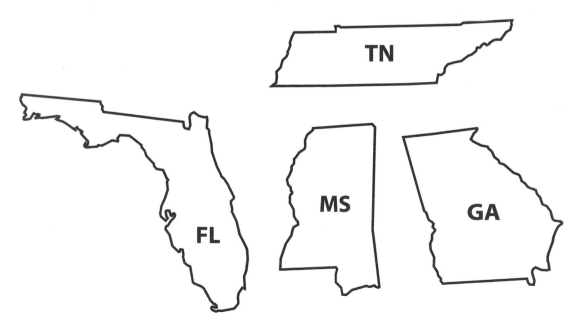

Ahoy, Matey!

The deep-water port of Mobile on the Gulf of Mexico is one of the main shipping ports in the nation and one of the busiest! Cotton shipped down the Tombigbee River on steamboats was the first major good to be shipped from Mobile. Then came iron and steel from Birmingham. Today, Mobile is a busy distribution point for goods, including coal and petroleum products.

When you're on board any kind of boat, you have to use special terms to talk about directions. Label the ship below with these terms:

> **bow:** front of the ship
> **stern:** back of the ship
> **fore:** towards the bow
> **aft:** towards the stern
> **port:** left as you face the bow
> **starboard:** right as you face the bow

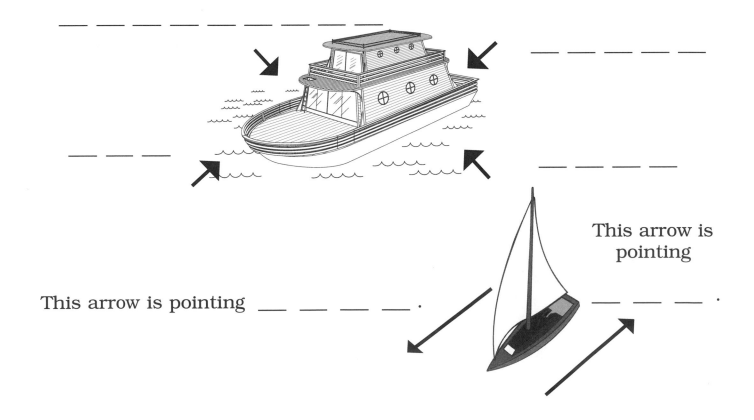

This arrow is pointing __ __ __ __ .

This arrow is pointing __ __ __ .

Alabama Politics As Usual!

Our elected government officials decide how much money is going to be spent on schools, roads, public parks, and libraries. Every election is important, and everyone who is eligible (able) to vote should do so! When you are 18 and register according to Alabama laws, you can vote! So please do! Your vote counts!

Today, many elected government officials are women. However, before the 19th Amendment to the U.S. Constitution, women were unable to vote in national elections! In 1920, enough states ratified the 19th Amendment, and it became the law of the land. Women gained total suffrage nationally and continue to be a major force in the election process today.

During the civil rights movement of the 1950s and '60s, many courageous people such as Dr. Martin Luther King, Jr. and Coretta Scott King fought for voting rights for *all* Americans. Finally, in 1965, the Voting Rights Act banned the unfair poll tax, literacy test, and property requirements that had previously kept African Americans from registering to vote.

On the lines provided, write down a question for each of the answers below. A hint follows each answer.

1. Question: _____

   Answer: A draft of a law presented for review

   (Short for William!)

2. Question: _____

   Answer: The right to vote

   (Don't make us suffer!)

3. Question: _____

   Answer: The ability to forbid a bill or law from being passed

   (Just say no!)

4. Question: _____

   Answer: The fundamental law of the United States that was

   framed in 1787 and put into effect in 1789

   (Alabama has one too!)

5. Question: _____

   Answer: An amendment

   (It's not something subtracted from #4!)

ANSWERS: (may vary slightly) 1-What is a bill? 2-What is suffrage? 3-What is a veto? 4-What is the Constitution? 5-What is an addition to the Constitution called?

What Shall I Be When I Grow Up?

Here are just a few of the jobs that kept early Alabamians busy.

Lawyer	Cooper (barrelmaker)	Tailor
Tenant Farmer	Carpenter	Minister
Woodcarver	Weaver	Baker
Judge	Barber	Pharmacist
Housekeeper	Gardener	Gaoler (jailer)
Silversmith	Mantuamaker (dressmaker)	Fisherman
Politician	Printer	Doctor
Dairyman	Cook	Milliner (hatmaker)
Wheelwright	Musician	Soldier
Teacher	Bookbinder	Hunter
Servant	Laundress	Blacksmith
Cabinetmaker	Jeweler	Sailor
Mayor	Innkeeper	Beekeeper
Plantation Owner	Stablehand	Gunsmith

You are a young colonist trying to decide what you want to be when you grow up.

Choose a career and next to it write a description of what you think you would do each day as a:

Write your career choice here!
_____

_____
_____
_____

Write your career choice here!
_____

_____
_____
_____

Write your career choice here!
_____

_____
_____
_____

Write your career choice here!
_____

_____
_____
_____

Governor of Alabama!

The governor is the leader of the state.

You've been assigned to write a biography of the governor of Alabama.

Before you can start your book, you need to jot down some notes in your trusty computer. Fill in the necessary information in the spaces provided on the dossier!

GOVERNOR'S NAME:

_____

_____

Date of Birth: _____

Place of Birth: _____

Father: _____

Mother: _____

Siblings: _____

Spouse: _____

Children: _____

Pets: _____

Schools Attended: _____

Previous Occupation(s): _____

Likes: _____

Dislikes: _____

abc • APPLICATIONS   MENU   CALCULATOR   FIND   123 •

The ORIGINAL Alabama Natives!

Until recently, scientists believed that the first humans came to North America about 14,000 years ago. These people crossed over a land bridge between Siberia and Alaska, and then spread out across the North American continent. New evidence now suggests that people may have first arrived at the Americas 15,000, 20,000 or even 30,000 years ago!

These prehistoric people were ancestors of the cliff-dwellers and mound builders that lived in present-day Alabama. These early people were nomadic hunters who traveled in small bands. They camped when seasons offered hunting, fishing, and fruit and nut gathering. Around AD 1000, farming began to replace hunting as the way of life for these early Alabamians.

What kinds of things did Native Americans use in their everyday life? For each of the things shown, circle YES if Native Americans did use it, or NO if they didn't.

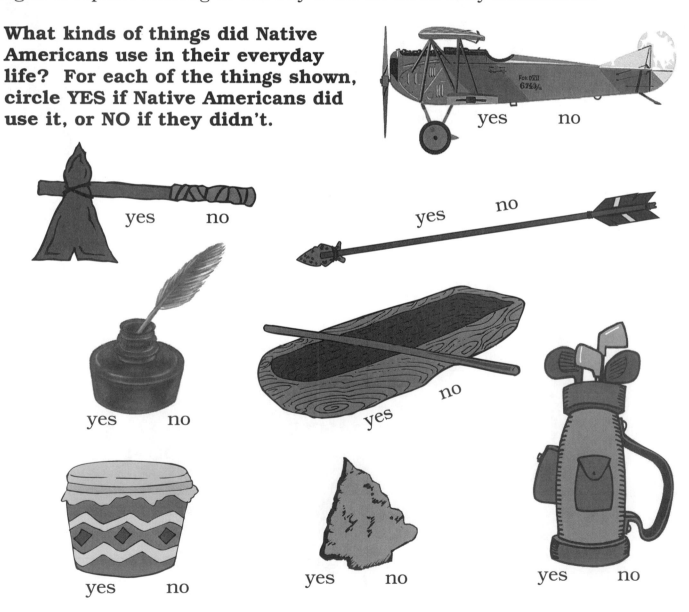

yes   no

yes   no

yes   no

yes   no

yes   no

yes   no

yes   no

yes   no

States All Around Code-Buster!

Decipher the code and write in the names of the states that border Alabama.

A B C D E F G H I J K L M N O P Q R

S T U V W X Y Z

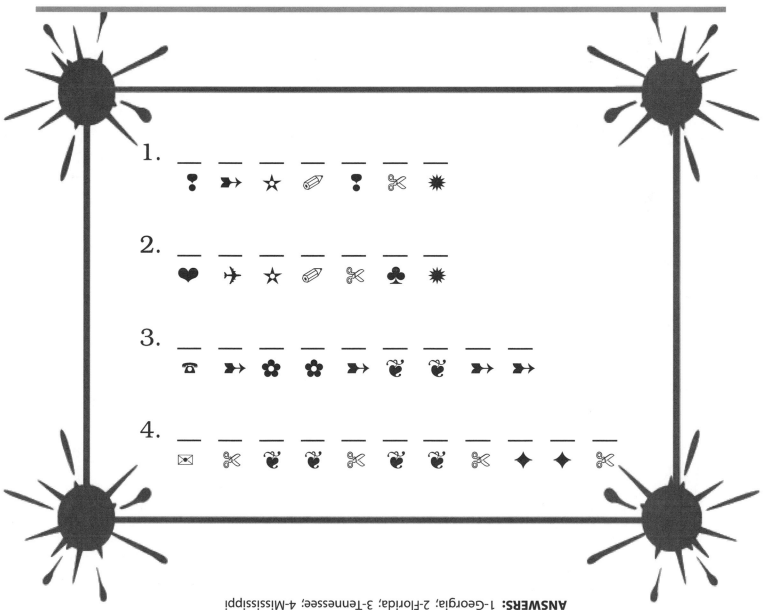

1. _ _ _ _ _ _ _

2. _ _ _ _ _ _ _

3. _ _ _ _ _ _ _ _ _

4. _ _ _ _ _ _ _ _ _ _ _

Unique Alabama Place Names!

Can you figure out the compound words that make up the names of these Alabama places?

Allgood

_____ _____

Bellwood

_____ _____

Bigbee

_____ _____

Brierfield

_____ _____

Campbell

_____ _____

Castleberry

_____ _____

Chestnut

_____ _____

Cottonwood

_____ _____

Evergreen

_____ _____

Fairhope

_____ _____

Goodsprings

_____ _____

Millport

_____ _____

Rockwood

_____ _____

Shortleaf

_____ _____

Tensaw

_____ _____

Woodland

_____ _____

Looking For a Home in Alabama!

Starting with the first, circle every other letter (or number) to check out the wildlife of Alabama!

1. Alabama's state bird, the golden-winged woodpecker, is commonly called _ _ _ _ _ _ _ _ _ _ _ _ _ _. It makes Alabama its year-round home and lives in cities and rural areas.
(Y O E P L Q L A O E W G H Z A M M E M U E V R)

2. Alabama's mountains, rolling hills, fields, and forests are home to white-tailed deer, bobcat, beaver, muskrat, fox, and _ _ _ _ _ _ _ _. **(R O A F C E C S O M O A N)**

3. Mallard and other species of ducks, Canada geese, snow geese, and _ _ _ _ _ _ _ _ _ _ are migratory birds that stop by Alabama on their trips north or south!
(B E L O U S E G O E W E C S P E)

4. _ _ _ _ _ _ _ _ _ _ _ _ _ _, Alabama's conservation program, helps preserve and protect the state's abundance wildlife!
(F E O D R L E A V W E W R W P I O L X D)

5. Alabama is making great progress restoring the population of _ _ _ _ _ _ _ _ _ _, bluebirds, ospreys, great blue herons, and brown pelicans by preserving wild-nesting areas through state conservation programs! Way to go, Alabama!
(B E A O L S D E Q A L G I L R E K S)

6. Alabama's mild climate is a great place for trees to grow abundantly! There are more than _ _ _ different types of trees in Alabama! **(1 2 2 3 5)**

I Love Alabama, Weather or Not!

Alabama's summers are long and hot! The winters are usually mild. Snow may fall in the northern region but is rare in the southern coastal areas.

The record high temperature of 112°F (44°C) occurred on September 5, 1925, at Centreville. The coldest day in Alabama was January 30, 1966, at New Market when the temperature dropped to a frigid -27°F (-33°C).

On the thermometer gauges below, color the mercury red (°F) to show the hottest temperature ever recorded in Alabama. Color the mercury blue (°F) to show the coldest temperature ever recorded in Alabama.

Fast Facts

It's raining, it's pouring! Alabama gets plenty of rain year-round! Average annual precipitation ranges from about 53 inches (135 centimeters) in the northern regions to 65 inches (165 centimeters) along the coast.

Fast Facts

Floods (again), Hurricanes, and a Killer Tornado! In 1929, the Alabama-Tombigbee river system floods southern Alabama causing $6 million in damage. Shortly after in 1932, hurricanes and a tornado blast their way through Alabama bringing more devastation and death!

°F

120
110
100
90
80
70
60
50
40
30
20
10
0
10
20
30
40
50
60

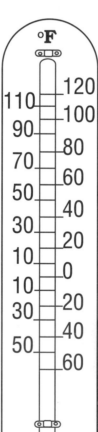

°F

120
110
100
90
80
70
60
50
40
30
20
10
0
10
20
30
40
50
60

Fast Facts

Capital Floods! In 1711, floods ravage original French capital of Fort Louis de la Mobile forcing settlers to move south and relocate the capital to present-day Mobile. In 1825, the Alabama River floods and devastates the capital city-today Cahaba. The capital moves once again, this time to Tuscaloosa.

The Scenic Route

Imagine that you've planned an exciting exploratory expedition around Alabama for your classmates. You've chosen some cities and other places to take your friends.

Circle these sites and cities on the map below, then number them in the order you would visit if you were traveling north to south through the state:

_____ **Lake Logan Martin** near Leeds

_____ **Museum of Fine Arts**, Montgomery

_____ **Church of St. Michael and All Angels**, Anniston

_____ **Gilliland-Reese Covered Bridge**, Gadsden

_____ **Oakleigh Period Museum House**, Mobile—features Antebellum Period House Museum, neoclassical-style home of Mobile merchant, James W. Roper

_____ **Russell Cave National Monument**, near Bridgeport

_____ **Talladega Superspeedway** near Pell City, a 2.66-mile (4.3-kilometer) tri-oval raceway that hosts the NASCAR races.

_____ **Jacksonville State University**

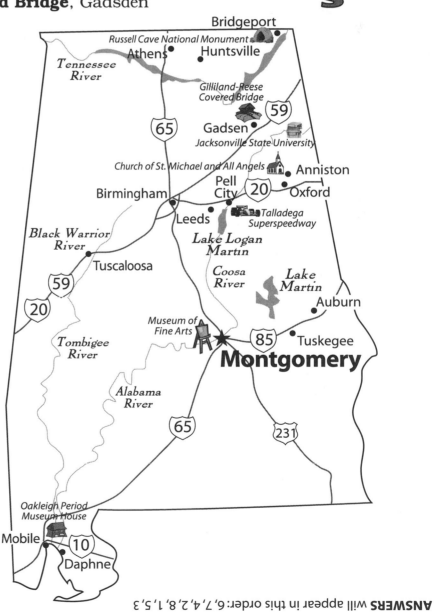

Key to a Map!

A map key, also called a map legend, shows symbols which represent different things on a map.

Match each word with a symbol for things found in the state of Alabama.

airport (Birmingham International Airport)

church (Christ Episcopal Church, Mobile) (Dexter Avenue King Memorial Baptist Church, Montgomery)

mountains (Cheaha Mountain)

lake (Lewis Smith Lake)

river (Tombigbee River)

road (I-65)

school (University of Alabama) (Auburn University)

state capital (Montgomery)

battle site (Fort Gaines Historic Site, Dauphin Island at Mobile Bay)

bird sanctuary (Eufaula National Wildlife Refuge)

BROTHER, CAN YOU SPARE A DIME?

After the collapse of the stock market on Wall Street in 1929, the state of Alabama, along with the rest of the nation, plunged headfirst into the Great Depression. It was the worst economic crisis America had ever known. Banks closed and businesses crashed...there was financial ruin everywhere.

Our President Helps

While the nation was in the midst of the Depression, Franklin Delano Roosevelt became president. With America on the brink of economic devastation, the federal government stepped forward and hired unemployed people to build parks, bridges, and roads. With this help, and other government assistance, the country began to slowly, and painfully, pull out of the Great Depression. Within the first 100 days of his office, Roosevelt enacted a number of policies to help minimize the suffering of the nation's many unemployed workers. These programs were known as the NEW DEAL. The jobs helped families support themselves and improved the country's infrastructure.

Alabama was especially hard hit by the Great Depression. Alabama was mostly an agricultural state and two-thirds of the farmers were tenant farmers who faced many challenges. In 1933, President Roosevelt and the U.S. government created many programs to help the nation and its citizens! The Tennessee Valley Authority was created to help control floods, improve navigation, produce electricity, reforest lands, and encourage agricultural and industrial development. This federal act greatly improved the everyday life of Alabama residents!

Put an X next to the jobs that were part of Roosevelt's New Deal.

1. computer programmer _____

2. bridge builder _____

3. fashion model _____

4. park builder _____

5. interior designer _____

6. hospital builder _____

7. school builder _____

8. website designer _____

ANSWERS: 2, 4, 6, 7

Alabama Newcomers

People have come to Alabama from other states and many other countries. As time goes by, Alabama's population grows more diverse. This means that people of different races and from different cultures and ethnic backgrounds have moved to Alabama. Alabamians benefits from their diverse culture as new residents bring a heritage rich in the traditions of their homelands.

In the past, many immigrants have come to Alabama from Spain, France, England, Ireland, Scotland, Germany, and Italy. Africans were "forcefully" migrated to Alabama. More recently, people have migrated to Alabama from Scandinavia, Greece, Laos, Vietnam, Cambodia, and China. Immigrants come in search of opportunities-jobs, education, or religious freedom. Only a certain number of immigrants are allowed to move to America each year. Many of these immigrants eventually become U.S. citizens.

Read the statement and decide if it's a fact or an opinion. Write your answer on the line.

1. Many of Alabama's early immigrants came from Europe.

2. Lots of immigrants speak a language other than English.

3. The clothing immigrants wear is very interesting.

4. Immigrants from Ireland have a neat accent when they speak.

5. Many immigrants will become United States citizens.

6. People have immigrated to Alabama from nearly every country in the world.

An immigrant is a person who migrates to another country in hopes of a better life.

ANSWERS: 1-fact; 2-fact; 3-opinion; 4-opinion; 5-fact; 6-fact

A Day in the Life of a Colonist!

Pretend you are a colonist in the days of early Alabama. You keep a diary of what you do each day. Write in the "diary" what you might have done on a long, hot summer day in July 1720.

This Old House!

Take yourself back 100 years. Can you imagine what life would be like in the Victorian Era? What did turn-of-the-century Alabamians own? How did they live?

See if you can pick out which of the following items people at the turn of the century had and which ones they did not.

Circle the things you might find or use around your 1900 home.

Home, Sweet Home!

Alabama has been the home of many different authors. Here are just a few. See if you can locate their hometowns on the map of Alabama below! **Write the number of each author near the town where he or she lived. Some towns may be used twice.**

1. Fannie Flagg—author, wrote *Fried Green Tomatoes at the Whistle Stop Cafe*; the movie, *Fried Green Tomatoes* was based on her book (home-Alabama's largest city, located near the intersection of I-20 and I-65)

2. Nelle Harper Lee—novelist, her only published novel was *To Kill a Mockingbird.* Harper Lee grew up in Alabama during the Great Depression. One childhood experience made quite an impact on her. The events from the Scottsboro Case formed the basis for Lee's Pulitzer Prize-winning novel, which was made into an Academy Award-winning movie and later into a powerful stage play. (home-located in Monroe Country in south central Alabama between Frisco City and Peterman)

3. Winston Groom—author, wrote *Forrest Gump*; made into Academy-Award-winning movie starring Tom Hanks (home-largest port city on Mobile Bay)

4. Mark Childress—author of *Joshua and Bigtooth* (home-Monroe County, neighbor to Harper Lee; not next-door neighbors, but lived in the same city)

5. Zelda Fitzgerald—author, books include *Save Me the Waltz and Bits of Paradise*; wife of F. Scott Fitzgerald who wrote several works including *The Great Gatsby*; (home-located at the intersection of I-65 and I-85 in south central Alabama)

6. Helen Friedman Blackshear—Alabama Poet Laureate; works include *Mother Was a Rebel, Southern Smorgasbord*, and *The Creek Captives and Other Alabama Stories* (home-located near I-20, southwest of Birmingham between Northport and Moundville)

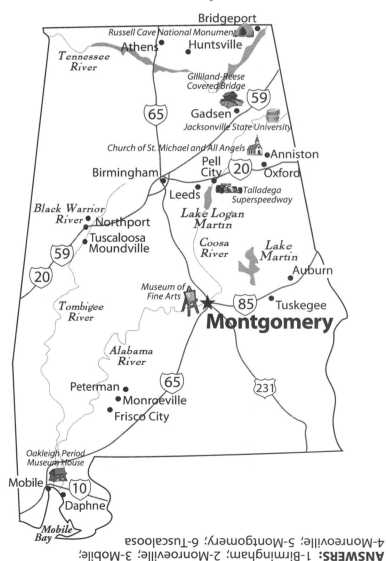

ANSWERS: 1-Birmingham; 2-Monroeville; 3-Mobile; 4-Monroeville; 5-Montgomery; 6-Tuscaloosa

Alabama Spelling Bee!

Good spelling is a good habit. Study the words on the left side of the page. Then fold the page in half and "take a spelling test" on the right side. Have a buddy read the words aloud to you. When finished, unfold the page and check your spelling. Keep your score. GOOD LUCK.

Each word is worth 5 points.

A perfect score is 100! How many did you get right?

Alabama _____

camellia _____

Cheaha _____

Cherokee _____

Chickasaw _____

Choctaw _____

civil rights _____

Confederacy _____

Creek _____

equality _____

flood _____

magnolia _____

Montgomery _____

peanuts _____

rocket _____

Shakespeare _____

Spain _____

steel _____

vote _____

yellowhammer _____

Naturally Alabama!

Fill in the bubblegram with some Alabama crops and natural resources. Use the letter clues to help you.

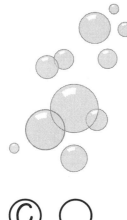
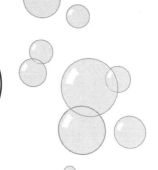

WORD BANK

Bauxite   Iron Ore
Coal   Limestone
Graphite   Marble
Gravel   Petroleum
Hematite   Sandstone

1. Ⓒ ◯ __ __ __

2. __ __ __ __ __ __ __ __

3. Ⓢ __ __ ◯ __ Ⓢ __ __ __ __

4. __ ◯ __ ◯ __ L __ __ __

5. __ __ __ Ⓥ __ __ __ __ __

6. G __ ◯ __ __ __ ◯ __

7. H __ __ __ __ __ __ __

8. __ __ __ __ ◯ __ __ __

9. __ __ __ M __ __ __ ◯ ◯ __ __

10. __ __ __ B __ __

Fast Facts

Did you know seafood is a natural resource, too? Most of Alabama's seafood catch comes from the Gulf of Mexico. Shrimp, oysters, blue crabs, and red snapper are important to Alabama's economy.

More than two-thirds of Alabama is covered by forests.

NATURAL RESOURCES: things that exist in or are formed by nature

Now unscramble the "bubble" letters to find out the mystery word!
HINT: What is one way we can help to save our environment?

__ __ __ __ __ __ __

ANSWERS: 1-coal; 2-iron ore; 3-sandstone; 4-petroleum; 5-gravel; 6-graphite; 7-hematite; 8-bauxite; 9-limestone; 10-marble

Gone Fishin'

The Tennessee Valley Authority and the U.S. Army Corps of Engineers created many of Alabama's lakes by building dams along the Tennessee, Coosa, Tallapoosa, and Chattahoochee rivers.

Put the names of some of Alabama's great lakes in alphabetical order by numbering them 1 to 10.

_____ Wheeler Lake

_____ Guntersville Lake

_____ Demopolis Lake

_____ Bankhead Lake

_____ Smith Reservoir

_____ Lake Jordan

_____ Logan Martin Lake

_____ Mitchell Lake

_____ Lay Lake

_____ Weiss Lake

All of Alabama's large lakes were formed by the construction of dams built to produce electric power.

Fast Facts RESERVOIR: a body of water stored for public use

ANSWERS will appear in this order: 10; 3; 2; 1; 8; 4; 6; 7; 5; 9

What a Great Idea!

Alabama has lots of great people with lots of great ideas! **See if you can fill in the blanks to figure out WHO came up with WHAT!**

1. _ _ _ _ _ _ _ _ _ _ was a silversmith who created a
_ _ _ _ _ _ _ _ _ _ _ _ _ _ _ for the _ _ _ _ _ _ _ _
Nation. He was the only man ever known to develop an alphabet on his own.

2. _ _ _ _ _ _ _ _ _ _ _ _ _ _ _ _ _ _ _ _ _ _ was an
educator and botanist recognized internationally for his agricultural
research. He developed hundreds of products from peanuts and sweet
potatoes. He served as director of the Department of Agricultural Research
at Tuskegee Institute. He received the NAACP Spingarn Medal and the
Theodore Roosevelt Medal.

3. _ _ _ _ _ _ _ _ _ _ _ _ _ _ _ _ _ _ _ _ _ _ was a
physician and public health expert. He served as a U.S. Army officer
and was a pioneer in the elimination of yellow fever, malaria, and the
bubonic plague.

4. Robert Jemison Van de Graaff was a physicist who invented the
_ _ _ _ _ _ _ _ _ _ _ _ _ _ _ _ _ _ _ _ _ _ _, a device used
in nuclear research.

5. Dr. Luther Leonidas Hill was a surgeon who performed the first
_ _ _ _ _ _ _ _ _ _ _ _ _ _ _ _ in the Western Hemisphere
when he sutured a stab wound in a young boy's heart. The operation took
place in Montgomery in 1902.

ANSWERS: 1-Sequoyah, written language, Cherokee; 2-George Washington Carver; 3-William Crawford Gorgas; 4-electrostatic generator; 5-open heart surgery

Famous Alabamians Scavenger Hunt!

Here is a list of some of the famous people associated with our state. **Go on a scavenger hunt to see if you can "capture" a fact about each one. Use an encyclopedia, almanac, or other resource you might need. Happy hunting!**

Hank Aaron   _____

Bobby Allison   _____

William Wyatt Bibb   _____

Marva Collins   _____

N. Jan Davis   _____

W.C. Handy   _____

Joseph Henry Johnson   _____

Joe Louis   _____

Willie Mays   _____

Alexander McGillivray   _____

John Hunt Morgan   _____

Jesse Owens   _____

Rosa Parks   _____

Red Eagle   _____

David Satcher   _____

Ken Stabler   _____

Benjamin Sterling Turner   _____

George Wallace   _____

Hank Williams, Sr.   _____

Tammy Wynette   _____

Alabama State Reptile Lives!

Use the words in the word bank to fill in the blanks in this Alabama story. Some may be used more than once.

Alabama's state _ _ _ _ _ _ _ _, the Alabama red-bellied turtle lives only in Alabama! Alabama red-bellied turtles live in fresh or _ _ _ _ _ _ _ _ _ (partly-fresh and partly-salt water). Alabama red-bellied turtles live in the _ _ _ _ _ _ _ _ _ _ _ _ delta area. Some have been _ _ _ _ _ _ _ _ _ in the Little River State Park Lake and on _ _ _ _ _ _ _ _ _ _ _ _ _ _.

On a _ _ _ _ _ day, these Alabama _ _ _ _ _ _ _ _ _ may be seen sunning themselves on _ _ _ _.
Alabamians are working hard to _ _ _ _ _ _ _ _ their state reptile—it's on the _ _ _ _ _ _ _ _ _ _ _ _ species list!

Map of North America

This is a map of North America. Alabama is one of the 50 states.

Color the state of Alabama red.

Color the rest of the United States yellow. Alaska and Hawaii are part of the United States and should also be colored yellow.

Color Canada green. Color Mexico blue.

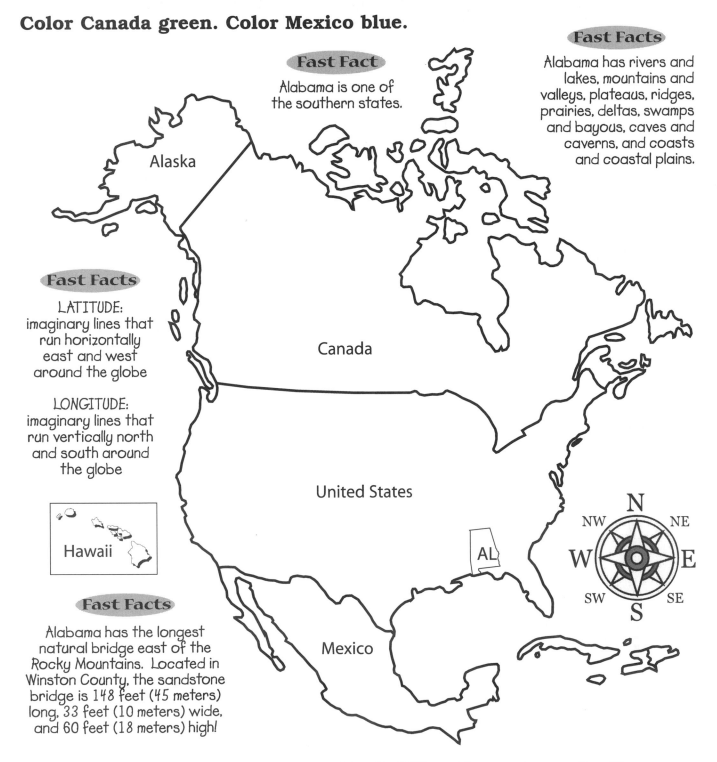

Fast Fact

Alabama is one of the southern states.

Fast Facts

Alabama has rivers and lakes, mountains and valleys, plateaus, ridges, prairies, deltas, swamps and bayous, caves and caverns, and coasts and coastal plains.

Fast Facts

LATITUDE: imaginary lines that run horizontally east and west around the globe

LONGITUDE: imaginary lines that run vertically north and south around the globe

Fast Facts

Alabama has the longest natural bridge east of the Rocky Mountains. Located in Winston County, the sandstone bridge is 148 feet (45 meters) long, 33 feet (10 meters) wide, and 60 feet (18 meters) high!

Alaska

Canada

United States

Hawaii

Mexico

AL

Rock 'n' Roll!

True or False?!

Alabama has an official gemstone, rock, and mineral! The star blue quartz is the official gemstone of Alabama. Quartz is the most common silicate (glass mineral). Quartz is very hard and has many industrial uses. It's used to help make clocks and watches.

Alabama has a state rock. It's marble—a metamorphic rock that may be white, pink, gray, red, or black. Alabama's marble has been used in buildings all over the United States. Crushed marble is used in textiles, plastics, paints, and electrical insulation.

Hematite is Alabama's official state mineral. Hematite is also known as "red iron ore" and was once Alabama's most-developed "nonfuel" mineral. The mining of hematite, coal, and limestone helped make Birmingham an important industrial center.

Read each sentence, and decide if it is TRUE or FALSE. Write your answers on the lines provided.

1. Alabama has an official gemstone, rock, and mineral!

   _____

2. The sun-yellow quartz is the official gemstone of Alabama.

   _____

3. Quartz is used to help make clocks and watches.

   _____

4. Alabama has a state rock. It's hematite!

   _____

5. Alabama has an official state mineral. It's marble!

   _____

ANSWERS: 1-true; 2-false; 3-true; 4-false; 5-false

Plague Turns To Profit!

In 1915, ball weevils eat there way through Alabama and dsetroy the cotton crop and the economy! The plaque turns to profit as farmers are forced to plant other crops including peanuts. Today, Alabama is on of the leading peanut-producing states in the nation!

A monument dedicated to the boll weevil is located in the toun of Enterprise. It acknowledges the roll this destructive little insect played in encouraging farmers to grow crpso other than cotton.

In the paragraph about important people from Alabama below there are eight misspelled words. Circle the misspelled words, and then spell them correctly on the lines provided.

_____   _____

_____   _____

_____   _____

Virtual Alabama!

It's time to build your own website! We've given you pictures of things that have to do with Alabama. Color and cut them out, and arrange them on a blank piece of paper to create a web page that will make people want to visit Alabama!

A Woman of Vision!

Helen Keller was born on June 27, 1880, in Tuscumbia, Alabama—healthy and energetic. At 18 months, a fever left her blind and deaf. Helen was an unruly child alone in a dark, silent "no world." A day in March 1887 was "the most important day she remembered in all her life." Miss Annie Sullivan, the miracle worker, arrived.

Helen's parents, Captain Arthur H. and Kate Keller, hired Miss Sullivan to find a way to reach Helen. And reach Helen she did! William Gibson wrote the award-winning play, *The Miracle Worker*, that told the story of how "Teacher" taught Helen to "talk."

Helen Keller learned to write, to speak, to read lips—she even learned foreign languages! Helen graduated cum laude in 1904 from Radcliffe College, the first deaf-blind person in history to graduate from college!

Helen spent the rest of her life helping others—the poor, the disabled. She fought for women's rights and equal rights for minorities, for worker's rights, and social issues. She wrote 13 books, contributed to magazines and newspapers, became a spokesperson for the American Foundation for the Blind, and lectured in many countries across the globe!

Read each sentence, and decide if it is TRUE or FALSE. Write your answers on the lines provided.

1. Helen Keller was born a normal, healthy child. A fever left her blind and deaf. _____

2. Helen never learned to read. _____

3. Miss Annie Sullivan was Helen's nurse.

   _____

4. Helen Keller learned to write, to speak, to read lips—she even learned foreign languages! She spent her life writing, teaching, and helping others! _____

ANSWERS: 1-true; 2-false; 3-false; 4-true

A River Runs Through It!

RIVER BANK

Alabama   Black Warrior
Choctawhatchee   Conecuh
Tombigbee

Fast Facts

Alabama has more than 1,600 miles (2,575 kilometers) of navigable water. Only the state of California has more navigable river miles than Alabama!

The Cahaba River is Alabama's most floated river!

---

1. _ _ _ _ _ _ _ River: This river shares the state's name!

2. The _ _ _ _ _ _ _ _ _ _ _ _ River was named in honor of Chief Tuscaloosa, a famous Choctaw leader.

3. Any Tom, Dick, or Harry would know this big river:
   _ _ _ _ _ _ _ _ _ River

4. Cone*huh*? _ _ _ _ _ _ _ River

5. You never know "what" you might "c" on this river:
   _ _ _ _ _ _ _ _ _ _ _ _ _ _ River

Alabama Firsts!

Want to learn how to fly?
The world's first flying school was founded at Maxwell Air Force Base near Montgomery by Orville and Wilbur Wright in 1910.

She Wins!
Lurleen Burns Wallace, wife of former governor George Wallace, became the first woman governor of Alabama when she was elected in 1967.

Celebrate!
Alabama first brought Mardi Gras to the western world during the 1700s. Mardi Gras is held on Shrove Tuesday, the day before Lent begins.

Is that land I see?
Alonso Álvarez de Piñeda was the first Spanish explorer to see Alabama. He sailed into Mobile Bay in 1519.

Way to go,
In 1936, track-and-field-champion Jesse Owens became the first American to win four Olympic gold medals.

Ding, ding, ding went the trolley!
In 1886, the world's first electric trolley system was introduced in Montgomery.

Fly Me to the Moon...
Alabamians built the first rocket to put astronauts on the moon.

Which "first" happened first?

- First trolley ride

- Jesse Owens wins Olympic gold medal.

- First flying lessons

The first "first" is:

_____

Alabama Gazetteer

A gazetteer is a list of places. For each of these famous Alabama places, write down the town in which it's located, and one interesting fact about the place. You may have to use an encyclopedia, almanac, or other resource to find the information, so dig deep!

1. Sloss Furnaces National Historic Landmark

   _____

2. Civil Rights Memorial

   _____

3. Looney's Amphitheatre and Riverboat

   _____

4. Museum of Art

   _____

5. Dismals Canyon

   _____

6. Alabama Music Hall of Fame

   _____

7. Old Cahawba Archaeological Park

   _____

8. Confederate Memorial Park

   _____

WORD BANK

Birmingham	Double Springs	Huntsville
Marbury	Montgomery	Phil Campbell
Selma	Tuscumbia	

Colonial Corn Husk Doll

You can make a corn husk doll similar to the dolls Alabama colonists' children played with! Here's how:

You will need:
- corn husks (or strips of cloth)
- string
- scissors

1. **Select a long piece of corn husk and fold it in half. Tie a string about one inch (2.54 centimeters) down from the fold to make the doll's head.**

2. **Roll a husk and put it between the layers of the tied husk, next to the string. Tie another string around the longer husk, just below the rolled husk. Now your doll has arms! Tie short pieces of string at the ends of the rolled husk to make the doll's hands.**

3. **Make your doll's waist by tying another string around the longer husk.**

4. **If you want your doll to have legs, cut the longer husk up the middle. Tie the two halves at the bottom to make feet.**

5. **Add eyes and a nose to your doll with a marker. You could use corn silk for the doll's hair.**

Now you can make a whole family of dolls!

Alabama Timeline!

A timeline is a list of important events and the year that they happened. You can use a timeline to understand more about history.

Read the timeline about Alabama history, then see if you can answer the questions at the bottom.

1763   Treaty of Paris ends French and Indian War, France gives Alabama to England.

1783   England cedes northern part of Alabama to United States and cedes Mobile region to Spain.

1819   Alabama joins Union, becomes 22nd state.

1861   Alabama secedes from the Union, becomes the Republic of Alabama for a short time, then joins the Confederate States of America.

1865   Confederacy surrenders to the Union, Civil War ends.

1868   Alabama is readmitted to the Union.

1964   Civil Rights Act passes.

1965   Voting Rights Act passes.

1986   Guy Hunt is elected governor-first Republican to lead Alabama since Reconstruction.

1. If you are a Republican celebrating Guy Hunt's election as governor, the year is _____.
2. If you've just attended a rally celebrating statehood, the year is _____.
3. If you're relieved that the Civil War is finally over, the year is _____.
4. If you're a legislator who's just voted for the Civil Rights Act, the year is _____.
5. If you've just been appointed to an office in the brand-new Republic of Alabama, the year is _____.

ANSWERS: 1-1986; 2-1819; 3-1865; 4-1964; 5-1861

Alabama State Economy!

Alabama banks provide essential financial services.

Some of the services that banks provide include:
- They lend money to consumers to purchase goods and services such as houses, cars, and education.
- They lend money to producers who start new businesses.
- They issue credit cards.
- They provide savings accounts and pay interest to savers.
- They provide checking accounts.

Circle whether you would have more, less, or the same amount of money after each event.

1. You deposit your paycheck into your checking account.   MORE   LESS   SAME

2. You put $1,000 in your savings account.   MORE   LESS   SAME

3. You use your credit card to buy new school clothes.   MORE   LESS   SAME

4. You borrow money from the bank to open a toy store.   MORE   LESS   SAME

5. You write a check at the grocery store.   MORE   LESS   SAME

6. You transfer money from checking to savings.   MORE   LESS   SAME

Service industries provide many jobs for Alabamians.

Tourism brings in more than $3 billion to Alabama's economy every year!

ANSWERS: 1.more 2.more 3.less 4.more 5.less 6.same

I Am A Famous Person From Alabama

From the Word Bank, find my name and fill in the blank.

WORD BANK

Alva Smith Belmont
Paul "Bear" Bryant
Nat "King" Cole
Pierre le Moyne, Sieur d'Iberville
Booker T. Washington

1. I was born a slave in Virginia but became an educator, author, and lecturer. I organized Tuskegee Institute and the National Negro Business League. I worked for economic equality for African Americans through education and employment.
Who am I? _____

2. I was a recognized authority on architecture who worked to improve hospitals, abolish child labor, improve conditions for women, and gain suffrage for women. I founded the Political Equality Association and established the first agricultural training school for women.
Who am I? _____

3. I and my brother, Jean-Baptiste Le Moyne, Sieur de Bienville, were sent by King Louis XIV of France to govern the Louisiana Territory. We landed on Dauphin Island in Mobile Bay in 1699. We established the territorial capital, Fort Louis de la Mobile, in 1702.
Who am I? _____

4. I was one of America's greatest college football coaches. I coached the University of Alabama's Crimson Tide for many winning seasons!
Who am I? _____

5. I was a singer and musician who was known as the "man with the velvet voice." I was the first African American performer to have a radio program and national television show.
Who am I? _____

ANSWERS: 1-Booker T. Washington; 2-Alva Smith Belmont; 3-Pierre le Moyne, Sieur d'Iberville; 4-Paul "Bear" Bryant; 5-Nat "King" Cole

Mounds Abound In Alabama!

Moundville Archaeological Park is one of the largest mound villages in North America. It's located on the Black Warrior River south of Tuscaloosa.

During the 12th and 13th centuries Moundville was a trade and cultural center for people of the Mississippian Culture. By 1350, the mound builders began to disappear, but they left artifacts such as tools, jewelry, and weapons for present-day archaeologists to uncover!

You are an archaeologist digging at Moundville. Below are pictures of some of the artifacts that you find. Now, you have to identify these strange objects and their uses. Write down what you think these things are for!

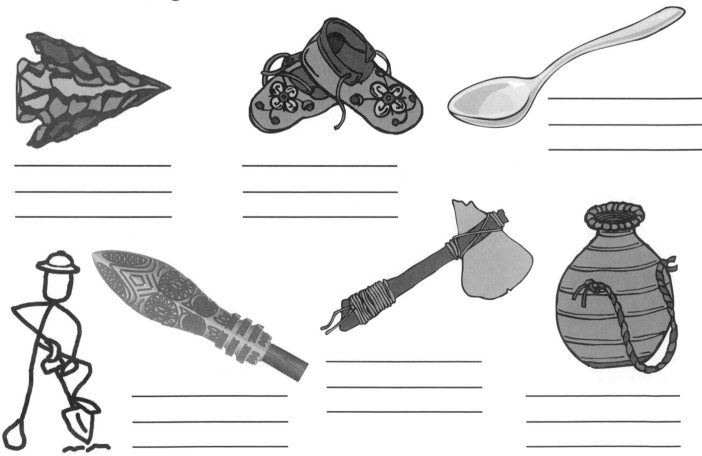

Alabama Native Americans!

When the colonists arrived in Alabama, there were several Native American groups already living there-Creek, Choctaw, Chickasaw, and Cherokee.

The Cherokee lived in the northeastern corner of the state, east of the Tennessee River. The Creek inhabited east-central and southern Alabama. The Chickasaw made northwestern Alabama their home, and the Choctaw lived in west-central Alabama, south of Moundville.

The U.S. government acquired land through treaties that forced Native Americans to cede (give up) their lands and move west to Indian Territory.

Draw a line from each group to its location on the map.

Creek

Choctaw

Chickasaw

Cherokee

IT'S MONEY IN THE BANK!!

You spent the summer working as a tour guide at DeSoto State Park along the Little River Canyon. You made a lot of money...$500 to be exact! **Solve the math problems below.**

TOTAL EARNED: $500.00

I will pay back my Mom this much for money I borrowed when I first started working. Thanks, Mom!   A. $20.00

      subtract A from $500   B. _____

I will give my little brother this much money for taking my phone messages while I was at work: C. $10.00

      subtract C from B   D. _____

I will spend this much on a special treat or reward for myself: E. $25.00

      subtract E from D   F. _____

I will save this much for college: G. $300.00

      subtract G from F   H. _____

I will put this much in my new savings account so I can buy school clothes: I. $100.00

      subtract I from H   J. _____

TOTAL STILL AVAILABLE
         (use answer J)   _____

TOTAL SPENT   (add A, C, and E)   _____

Take A Tour Of These Terrific Alabama Towns!

Find the names of these Alabama cities in the Word Search below:

```
Z O N E D S D A G W K X W D Y
N N S K U D A P H N E E A E R
H U N T S V I L L E S C S N E
J W E H Q Q N S M A E N A T M
J A C K S O N V I L L E K E O
M A H G N I M R I B I R C R G
F A I R F I E L D V B O I P T
N O T S I N N A N W O L H R N
D E C A T U R M X I M F C I O
E E B B U H C E H C T A H S M
O R O B S T T O C S R R S E Y
```

Numbering the Alabamians!

STATE OF ALABAMA
CENSUS REPORT

Every ten years, it's time for Alabamians to stand up and be counted. Since 1790, the United States has conducted a census, or count, of each of its citizens. **Practice filling out a pretend census form.**

Name _____ Age [ ]

Place of Birth _____

Current Address _____

Does your family own or rent where you live? _____

How long have you lived in Alabama? _____

How many people are in your family? _____

How many females? [ ]   How many males? [ ]

What are their ages? _____

How many rooms are in your house? [ ]

How is your home heated? _____

How many cars does your family own? [ ]

How many telephones are in your home? [ ]

Is your home a farm? _____

Sounds pretty nosy, doesn't it? But a census is very important. The information is used for all kinds of purposes, including setting budgets, zoning land, determining how many schools to build, and much more. The census helps Alabama leaders plan for the future needs of its citizens. Hey, that's you!!

Endangered And Threatened Alabama!

Each state has a list of the endangered species found within its borders. An animal is labeled endangered when it is at risk of becoming extinct, or dying out completely. Land development, changes in climate and weather, and changes in the number of predators are all factors that can cause an animal to become extinct. Today many states are passing laws to help save animals on the endangered species list.

Can you help rescue these endangered and threatened animals by filling in their names below?

WORD BANK

> Alabama beach mouse
> cavefish
> red-bellied turtle
> American peregrine falcon
> West Indian manatee

1. Alabama c _ _ _ _ f _ _ _

2. _ m _ _ _ _ _ _ p _ _ _ _ _ _ n _ _ _ _ c _ _

3. A _ _ _ _ _ _ _ _ e _ _ _ _ _ u _ _

4. Alabama _ _ _ - _ _ _ _ _ _ _ turtle

5. _ _ s _ _ _ d _ _ _ _ _ n _ t _ _ _

Circle the animal that is extinct (not here anymore).

Fast Facts

Plants can be endangered, too! Alabama's carnivorous green pitcher plant is endangered! Carnivorous means it eats meat (like insects). That's a switch—a plant eating the insect instead of the insect eating the plant!

ANSWERS: 1-Alabama cavefish; 2-American peregrine falcon; 3-Alabama beach mouse; 4-Alabama red-bellied turtle; 5-West Indian manatee

Sing A State Song!

Here's the first and last verses of Alabama's state song. **Read or sing it, then answer the questions about this great state song!**

"Alabama"

words by Julia Strudwick Tutwiler
music by Edna Goeckel Gussen

Alabama, Alabama
We will aye be true to thee,
From thy Southern shores where groweth,
By the sea thine orange tree.
To thy Northern vale where floweth,
Deep and blue thy Tennessee,
Alabama, Alabama
We will aye be true to thee!

Little, little, can I give thee,
Alabama, mother mine;
But that little-hand, brain, spirit,
As I have and am are thine,
Take, O take the gift and giver,
Take and serve thyself with me,
Alabama, Alabama,
I will aye be true to thee!

Answer the following questions:

1. What grows by the Southern shores?

_____

2. What flows in the Northern vale?

_____

3. What will we aye (always) be?

_____

4. What can the writer give to Alabama?

_____

5. What should Alabama do with the gift and giver?

_____

ANSWERS: (may vary slightly) 1-orange trees; 2-Tennessee River; 3-true to thee; 4-hand, brain, spirit; 5-take and serve thyself with me

Getting Ready To Vote in Alabama!

When you turn 18, you will be eligible to vote. Your vote counts! Many elections have been won by just a few votes. **The following is a form for your personal voting information. You will need to do some research to get all the answers!**

I will be eligible to vote on this date _____

I live in this Congressional District _____

I live in this State Senate District _____

I live in this State Representative District _____

I live in this Voting Precinct _____

The first local election I can vote in will be _____

The first state election I can vote in will be _____

The first national election I can vote in will be _____

The governor of our state is _____

One of my state senators is _____

One of my state representatives is _____

The local public office I would like to run for is _____

The state public office I would like to run for is _____

The federal public office I would like to run for is _____

Did you know that our state government has 35 senators?

The number of legislators may change after each census.

No, but I do know we have 105 representatives!

Alabama State Seal

The state seal of Alabama features two circles, a smaller one in the center of a larger one, with the words "Alabama Great Seal" between them. A map of Alabama showing the primary rivers, bordering states, and the Gulf of Mexico is inside the circles.

Fast Facts Alabama's state motto is *Audemus Jura Nostra Defendere.* That's Latin for We Dare Defend Our Rights.

Color the state seal.

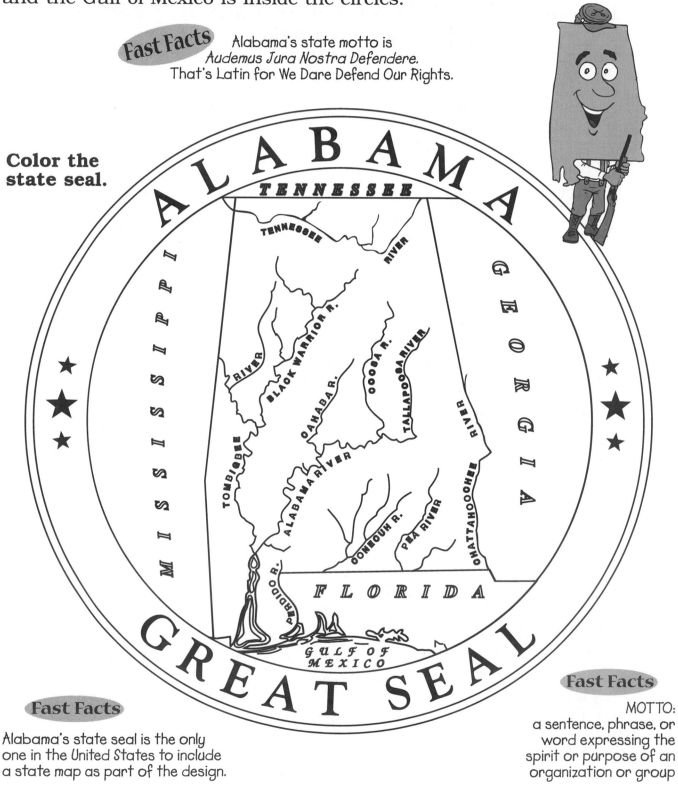

Fast Facts

Alabama's state seal is the only one in the United States to include a state map as part of the design.

Fast Facts

MOTTO: a sentence, phrase, or word expressing the spirit or purpose of an organization or group

Alabama State Symbol Scramble!

Unscramble the names of these symbols for the state of Alabama.
Write the answers in the word wheel around the picture of each symbol.

1. **N R E H T U O S   F A E L G N O L   E N I P**   *HINT:* Alabama's state tree has needles that are bundled in "threes" and grow to about 1 foot (30 centimeters). The pine cones grow to about 7 inches (18 centimeters) long.
2. **A C E M L L A I**   *HINT:* The spectacular state flower blossoms for nine months of the year—even in winter, when few other plants are in bloom. Camellias can be red, white, or pink, or a mixture of these colors.
3. **C A P N E**   *HINT:* Alabama's state nut is tasty and a good source of vitamin B-6. Many southern recipes such as pralines and pies make good use of these great-tasting nuts!
4. **M O U T H L A R G E   S S B A**   *HINT:* The state freshwater fish is greenish with a dark side stripe and lives in Alabama's lakes, ponds, and rivers.
5. **R I A N C G K   H R E S O**   *HINT:* Alabama's official state horse is a very strong horse with a smooth, natural gait (or stride) and can sustain a fast pace for a long time. Racking horses are very comfortable to ride and are usually friendly to people.

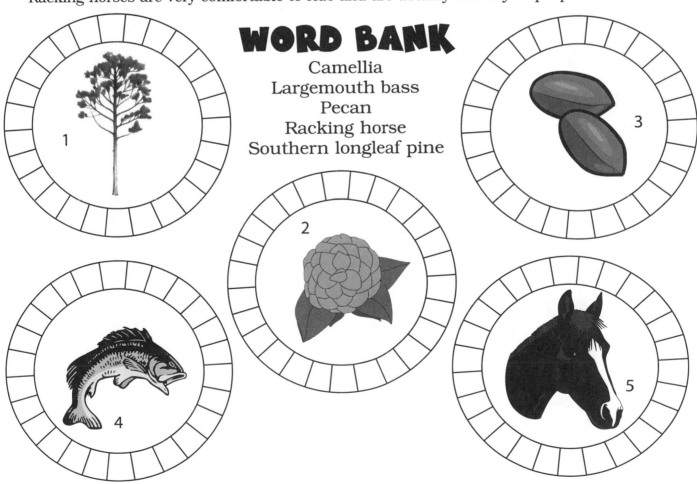

WORD BANK
Camellia
Largemouth bass
Pecan
Racking horse
Southern longleaf pine

ANSWERS: 1-Southern longleaf pine; 2-camellia; 3-pecan; 4-largemouth bass; 5-racking horse

A Quilt Of Many Counties

    Each of Alabama's 67 counties has a governing body to oversee county affairs. County officers include a probate judge, sheriff, clerk of the county court, superintendent of education, and health officials.

    Most towns and cities have a mayor and city council. Some of the larger cities have a commission and city manager to help with affairs of state!

– Label your county. Color it red.

– Label the counties that touch your county. Color them blue.

– Now color the rest of the counties green.

Civil Rights For All!

In 1955, Rosa Parks, an African American woman, took a very brave step toward integration and civil rights. After a long day at work, she took a seat on a Montgomery bus, but she wouldn't give it up to a white man as the law of segregation required. Rosa Parks was arrested, leading to a year-long boycott of Montgomery buses. Dr. Martin Luther King, Jr. led the successful boycott which ended in 1956 with a ruling from the U.S. Supreme Court outlawing all segregated public transportation in the city!

The Civil Rights Act of 1964 banned discrimination on the basis of color, race, national origin, religion or sex; guaranteed equal access to public facilities, the right to vote, and employment opportunities.

In 1965, Dr. Martin Luther King, Jr. led thousands in a march from Selma to Montgomery to protest unjust obstacles that kept African Americans from registering to vote. Dr. King's historic march led to the passage of the Voting Rights Act which banned the unfair poll tax, literacy test, and property requirements.

These hard-fought battles for civil rights raged for many years in Alabama. Today, the people of Alabama are working together to create a better future for all Alabamians!

Read each statement about this historical movement in Alabama and decide whether the statement is a FACT or an OPINION. Write your answer on the line.

1. Rosa Park was an African-American who took a brave step toward civil rights. _____

2. Dr. Martin Luther King, Jr. was an important leader in the civil rights movement. _____

3. The Civil Rights Act of 1964 was the most important U.S. legislative bill ever! _____

4. Before 1965 and the passage of the Voting Rights Act, the obstacles that kept African-Americans from registering to vote were very unjust! _____

ANSWERS: 1-fact; 2-fact; 3-opinion; 4-fact

Do You Believe In Ghosts?

As the ghostly story of the Red Lady of Huntingdon College goes...a young lady named Martha **attended** Huntingdon College in Montgomery in the early 1900s. Martha wasn't happy at Huntingdon College, but her **powerful** father forced her to stay.

Martha loved the color red. She dressed in red from head to toe, and **decorated** her dorm room all in red.

Martha was unhappy and shy, and she acted pretty strange—so she didn't have any friends. Martha was so unhappy that she finally took her own life by cutting her wrists open. The college president became worried because she had not seen Martha for awhile and was **horrified** to find her dead, in a pool of blood in her dorm room.

To this day, Martha still walks the halls of Huntingdon College dressed all in red! On her birthday each year, an **eerie** red glow can be seen in her room!

Figure out the meaning of these words from the story above.

1. attended:

   _____

2. powerful:

   _____

3. decorated:

   _____

4. horrified:

   _____

5. ccric:

   _____

HINT: You may need to look for the root word.

Now check your answers in a dictionary. How close did you get to the real definitions?

Which Hall Of Famer Am I?

From the Word Bank, find my name and fill in the blank.

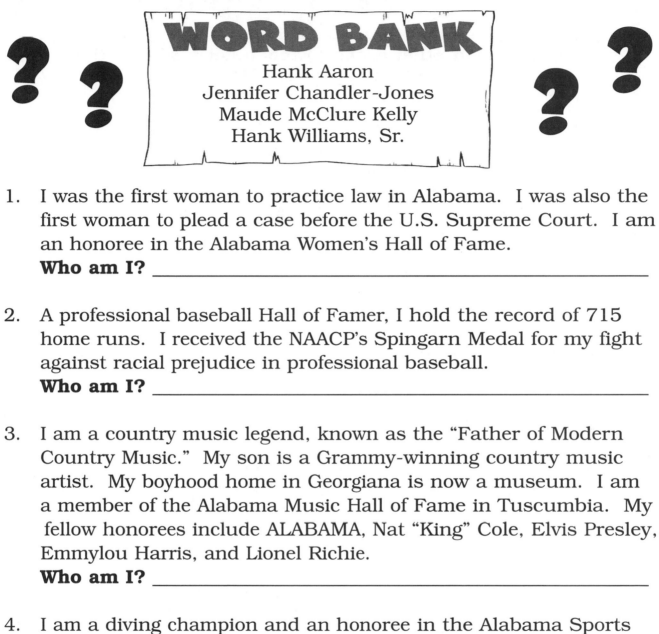

WORD BANK

Hank Aaron
Jennifer Chandler-Jones
Maude McClure Kelly
Hank Williams, Sr.

1. I was the first woman to practice law in Alabama. I was also the first woman to plead a case before the U.S. Supreme Court. I am an honoree in the Alabama Women's Hall of Fame.
   Who am I? _____

2. A professional baseball Hall of Famer, I hold the record of 715 home runs. I received the NAACP's Spingarn Medal for my fight against racial prejudice in professional baseball.
   Who am I? _____

3. I am a country music legend, known as the "Father of Modern Country Music." My son is a Grammy-winning country music artist. My boyhood home in Georgiana is now a museum. I am a member of the Alabama Music Hall of Fame in Tuscumbia. My fellow honorees include ALABAMA, Nat "King" Cole, Elvis Presley, Emmylou Harris, and Lionel Richie.
   Who am I? _____

4. I am a diving champion and an honoree in the Alabama Sports Hall of Fame in Birmingham. I won an Olympic gold medal and was quoted as saying, "Winning the Olympic medal is much more than an individual achievement." My fellow honorees include Coach Paul "Bear" Bryant, Joe Louis, Jesse Owens, Joe Namath, and Bobby Allison.
   Who am I? _____

ANSWERS: 1-Maude McClure Kelly; 2-Hank Aaron; 3-Hank Williams, Sr.; 4- Jennifer Chandler-Jones

It Could Happen— And It Did!

These historical events from Alabama's past are all out of order. Can you put them back together in the correct order? Number these events from 1 to 10, beginning with the earliest. (There's a great big hint at the end of each sentence.)

____ More than 200,000 meteors per hour flew through the sky as Mother Nature treated Alabama to an amazing astronomical fireworks display! (1833)

____ The spectacular camellia became the state flower of Alabama. (1959)

____ The Scottsboro Case involved a conflict between whites and blacks on a train. The black men were arrested, falsely charged, and sentenced to death. The legal ordeal lasted six years and went to the U.S. Supreme Court-twice! The defendants were finally freed. (1931)

____ The nation's first wave pool was built at Point Mallard Park in Decatur. (1970)

____ Birmingham iron ore was used to cast the statue of Vulcan, the Roman god of fire, that stands on top of Red Mountain. It's one of the largest cast-iron structures ever made! (1904)

____ Alabama's present state constitution was adopted. (1901)

____ William Wyatt Bibb became the first state governor of Alabama and helped form the state government. (1819)

____ The Alabama red-bellied turtle was designated the state reptile. (1990)

____ Alabama's lowest temperature, -27°F (-33°C), occurred in New Market. (1966)

____ Alabama's hottest temperature, 112°F (44°C), occurred in Centreville. (1925)

ANSWRS will appear in the following order: 2; 7; 6; 9; 4; 3; 1; 10; 8; 5

Rocket City, USA!

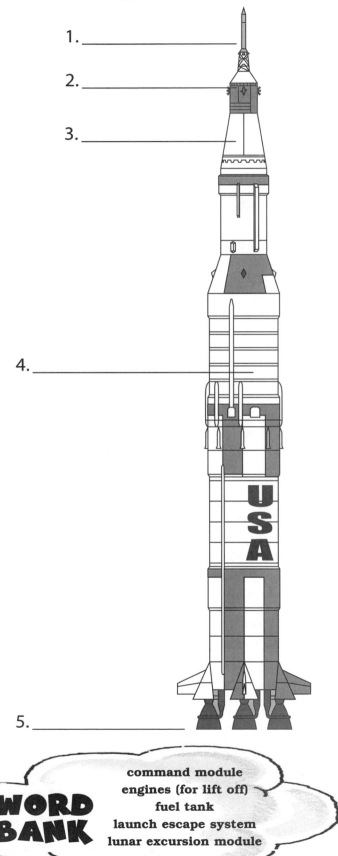

In 1960, the United States wanted to explore the final frontier—space! The George C. Marshall Space Flight Center was built in Huntsville. It was the first headquarters of NASA, the National Aeronautics and Space Administration. Huntsville and its research labs, assembly plants, and launch pads became known as Rocket City, USA!

Huntsville's U.S. Space and Rocket Center offers an up-close look at rockets, spaceships, shuttles, lunar landing vehicles, and moon rocks. Visitors can ride the Space Shot, a heart-pounding 4-G ride up a 180-foot (55-meter) tower to experience a few seconds of weightlessness- just like real space!

The ultimate "mission" includes a trip to Space Camp, where for five days kids of all ages (even grownups) can experience astronaut-training activities to find out what astronauts do in space. "Astronauts for the day" even go on a "pretend" space shuttle mission!

You can be an "Astronaut for the day" right now! **Check out the rocket and label the different parts. Maybe it will be the beginning of a great career!**

1._____

2._____

3._____

4._____

5._____

WORD BANK

command module
engines (for lift off)
fuel tank
launch escape system
lunar excursion module

ANSWERS: 1-launch escape system; 2-command module; 3-lunar excursion module; 4-fuel tank; 5-engines (for lift off)

Word Wheel labels: Auburn University, Dancing Rabbit Creek, Alibamu, Montgomery, Oak Mountain, **Word Wheel**, Mobile, Montgomery Zoo, Tuscumbia, Tuskegee, Selma

Alabama Word Wheel—Give It Another Spin!

Using the Word Wheel of Alabama names, complete the sentences below.

1. Alabama got its name from a Creek tribe, the _ _ _ _ _ _ _ _, that once lived in the area. Alabama means "I clear the thicket" and refers to the tribe's method of clearing land to plant crops.

2. Huntsville, Cahaba, and Tuscaloosa served as capitals of Alabama from 1819 until 1846 when _ _ _ _ _ _ _ _ _ _ _ became the permanent state capital!

3. In March 1780, during the Revolutionary War, Bernardo de Galvez, the governor of Florida and Louisiana captured the British post at _ _ _ _ _ _. The battle took only two days to win!

4. In 1830, the treaty of _ _ _ _ _ _ _ _ _ _ _ _ _ _ _ _ _ _ _ _ _ forced the Choctaw to cede their lands. The tribe gathered for three days to mourn and grieve before they left their ancestral homeland.

5. Local citizens supported the building of the _ _ _ _ _ _ _ _ Institute. They donated their time, materials, and effort to make the school a reality.

6. John William Heisman was a successful and well-known football coach at _ _ _ _ _ _ _ _ _ _ _ _ _ _ _ _. The Heisman Trophy given to the most outstanding college football player is named in his honor.

7. *The Miracle Worker* is the State Outdoor Drama and is performed each summer at Ivy Green, Helen Keller's _ _ _ _ _ _ _ _ _ _ home. The pump where Helen realized W-A-T-E-R and everything else in the world has a name, is still on the grounds.

8. _ _ _ _ _ _ _ _ _ _ _ is Alabama's largest state park.

9. _ _ _ _ _ _ _ _ _ _ _ _ _ _ has rare animals with natural and man-made barriers that allow visitors an up-close view of the animals without cages.

10. _ _ _ _ _ _ to Montgomery March Byway follows the route of the 1965 march for voting rights led by Dr. Martin Luther King, Jr.

Alabama Pop Quiz!

Pop quiz! It's time to test your knowledge of Alabama! Try to answer all of the questions before you look at the answers.

1. Racking horses became popular in the 1800s on _____ when folks learned they could be ridden comfortably for hours.
   - a. southern plantations
   - b. the beach
   - c. trails in state parks

2. Which river is NOT an Alabama border?
   - a. Chattahoochee River
   - b. Perdido River
   - c. Tombigbee River

3. One of the leading characters in Harper Lee's famous novel *To Kill a Mockingbird* has a name that rhymes with "doubt."
   - a. Pout
   - b. Scout
   - c. Mouth

4. John Hollis Bankhead helped develop the first national _____ system.
   - a. school
   - b. library
   - c. automobile highway

5. Which is NOT a nickname for Montgomery ?
   - a. "birthplace of the blues"
   - b. "Capital of the Confederacy"
   - c. "birthplace of the civil rights movement"

6. What did Braxton Bragg Comer, Alabama's Education Governor, build in every county?
   - a. playground
   - b. high school
   - c. college

7. Lookout Mountain Parkway that runs from Gadsden to the Tennessee state line has waterfalls and _____
   - a. seashores
   - b. presidential monuments
   - c. covered bridges

8. Where are the National Speleological Society's headquarters located?
   - a. Huntsville
   - b. Montgomery
   - c. Birmingham

9. The only state with all the _____ needed to make iron and steel is Alabama.
   - a. manpower
   - b. government funding
   - c. major natural resources

10. Alabama was the _____ state to join the Union.
    - a. 32nd
    - b. 22nd
    - c. 42nd

ANSWERS: 1-a; 2-c; 3-b; 4-c; 5-a; 6-b; 7-c; 8-a; 9-c; 10-b

Strong As Steel!

Alabama is known for its iron- and steel-making industry. Hematite, or red iron ore, was mined for many years in central and northeastern Alabama. The abundance of hematite, coal, and limestone opened the way for Birmingham to become an important industrial center.

Today, iron and steel products are made in the triangle area formed by Birmingham, Decatur, and Gadsden. Raw ore is transformed into materials that become a part of our roads, rails, cars and trucks, and buildings.

Although Alabama is known for its iron- and steel-making industry, the state's leading manufactured goods are paper and pulp products. Chemical production is second among Alabama's manufactured products and textiles rank third. The manufacturing of metals comes in fourth.

In each pair of sentences below, one of the statements is false. Read them carefully and choose the sentence that is not true. Cross out the false sentence, and circle the true sentence.

1. Alabama is known for its iron- and steel-making industry. Hematite, or red iron ore, was mined for many years in southern Alabama.

2. Alabama has an abundance of hematite, coal, and limestone. The abundance of natural resources made Dothan an important industrial center.

3. Today, iron and steel products are made in the triangle area formed by Birmingham, Decatur, and Gadsden. Raw ore is transformed into foods and paper products.

4. Textiles ranks first among Alabama's manufactured goods. The manufacturing of metals comes in fourth.

ANSWERS: 1-second is false; 2-second is false; 3-second is false; 4-first is false

Covered In Covered Bridges

Alabama's historic beauty goes beyond magnificent homes and stately buildings. Grand old covered bridges remind travelers of years gone by as they cross Alabama's rivers, ponds, and creeks.

Let's visit some of Alabama's stately bridges. Some are new, some are old. Some were built as long ago as the mid-1850s.

Alamuchee-Bellamy Bridge, Livingston (built in 1861)
Old Easley Bridge, Oneonta (built in 1927)
Salem-Shotwell Bridge, Opelika (built in 1900)
Oakachoy Bridge, Equality (built in 1916)
Pumpkin Hollow Bridge, Sterrett (built in 1995)
Swann Bridge, Cleveland (built in 1933)

Using the information in the paragraphs above, graph the ages of the covered bridges. The first one has been done for you.

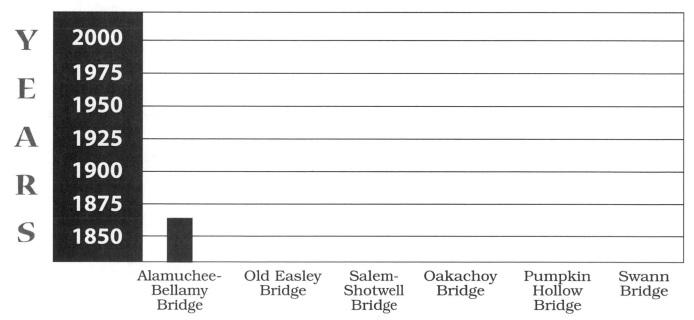

COVERED BRIDGES

What's In A Name? What's In A Haiku?

The state of Alabama got its name from a Creek tribe, the Alibamu, that once lived in the area. Alabama means "I clear the thicket" and refers to the tribe's method of clearing land to plant crops.

Many of Alabama's names, such as Chattahoochee, Chickasaw, Choctaw, and Cheaha, reflect the state's Native American heritage.

A *haiku* is a three-line poem with a certain number of syllables in each line. Look at the example below:

The first line has 5 syllables.
Al/a/ba/ma/state

The second line has 7 syllables.
Lots/of/love/ly/sights/are/great!

The third line has 5 syllables.
I/can/hard/ly/wait!

Now, write your own *haiku* about the amazing state of Alabama!

_____

_____

_____

Time For A Hike!

The state of Alabama is blessed with roaring rivers, lovely lakes, majestic mountains, wonderful waterfalls, and terrific trails. Everything a nature lover loves!

Throughout the state hikers will find many different trails to explore. Some are long. Some are short. Some are easy to climb. Some are hard. The "degree of difficulty" shows if the trail is easy or strenuous (really tough) to hike!

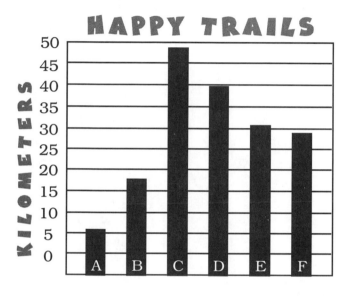

HAPPY TRAILS

Ⓐ **Alabama Reunion Trail**, 3.8 miles (6 kilometers) Wind Creek State Park

Ⓑ **Munny Sokol Park Trails**, 11 miles (18 kilometers) Tuscaloosa

Ⓒ **Black Warrior Horse Trails**, 30 miles (48 kilometers) Bankhead National Forest

Ⓓ **Sipsey Wilderness Trails**, 25 miles (40 kilometers) Bankhead National Forest

Ⓔ **Conecuh Trail**, 20 miles (32 kilometers) Conecuh National Forest

Ⓕ **Bump Trail,** 18 miles (29 kilometers) Oak Mountain State Park

Explore the chart for the answers to these questions:

1. The shortest trail on the chart is the _ _ _ _ _ _ _ _ _ _ _ _ _ _ _ _ _ _ which is __.__ miles (____ kilometers).

2. Which trails could you hike or ride your horse on?

   _ _ _ _ _ _ _ _ _ _ _ _ _ _ _ _ _ _ _ _ _ _ _

3. Which trail is closest to 21 miles? _ _ _ _ _ _ _ _ _ _ _ _

4. Which trail runs through Oak Mountain State Park for 18 miles (29 kilometers)? _ _ _ _ _ _ _ _ _

How Big is Alabama?

Alabama is the 30th largest state in the United States. It has an area of approximately 52,237 square miles (135,283 square kilometers).

Can you answer the following questions?

1. How many states are there in the United States?

   _____

2. How many states are smaller than our state?

   _____

3. How many states are larger than our state?

   _____

4. One mile = 5,280 ____ ____ ____ ____

   HINT:

5. Draw a square foot.

6. Classroom Challenge: After you have drawn a square foot, measure the number of square feet in your classroom. Most floor tiles are square feet (12 inches by 12 inches). How many square feet are in your classroom? _____

   Bonus: Try to calculate how many classrooms would fit in the total area of your state. _____

   Hint: About 46,464 average classrooms would fit in just one square mile!

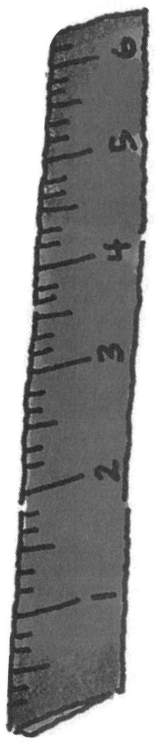

It's Time To Celebrate!

The Alabama Shakespeare Festival is one of the largest Shakespeare festivals in the world! It was founded in Anniston in 1972 and moved to Montgomery in 1985 when Winton and Carolyn Blount provided the money to build the new performing arts complex. A 200-acre (81-hectare) English-style park surrounds the building. *To be, or not to be...*

Alabama has many great celebrations! Visit these Alabama events to answer the questions below!

- Mardi Gras, Mobile
- Zoo Weekend, Montgomery
- Selma Pilgrimage Weekend
- Birmingham Festival of Arts
- W.C. Handy Music Festival, Florence
- Tennessee Valley Old Time Fiddlers Convention, Athens State College
- Gerhart Chamber Music Festival, Guntersville
- Birmingham Rose Show
- Alabama Renaissance Faire, Florence
- Chilton County Peach Festival, Clanton
- Diehard 500, Talladega
- River Boat Regatta, Guntersville
- South Alabama State Fair, Montgomery
- National Shrimp Festival, Gulf Shores
- National Peanut Festival, Dothan
- Native American Festival, Moundville

1. Your mother loves to listen to chamber music. You and your family are going to hear the beautiful notes played at the _ in Guntersville.

2. You cook up the best-tasting pot of boiled peanuts in Alabama. You and your nuts head to Dothan for _!

3. Your grandpa plays a mean fiddle! You're off to hear him play in the Tennessee Valley Old Time Fiddlers Convention at _ _ _ _ _ _ _ _ _ _ _ _ _ _ _ _ _ _.

4. Gentlemen, start your engines for the _ _ _ _ _ _ _ _ _ _ _ in Talladega!

ANSWERS: 1-Gerhart Chamber Music Festival; 2-National Peanut Festival; 3-Athens State College; 4-Diehard 500

"A" Is For The Awesome State of Alabama!

The words below are known as an acrostic.
Using each letter of Alabama's name, write a word or phrase that describes it. The first is done for you.

A is for all the beauty of Alabama!

L

A

B

A

M

A

Great Job!!!